www.EffortlessMath.com

... So Much More Online!

✓ FREE Math lessons

✓ More Math learning books!

✓ Mathematics Worksheets

✓ Online Math Tutors

Need a PDF version of this book?

Please visit www.EffortlessMath.com

FTCE General Knowledge Math Study Guide 2022 - 2023

Step-By-Step Guide to Preparing for the FTCE General Knowledge Math Test

By

Reza Nazari

All inquiries should be addressed to:
info@effortlessMath.com
www.EffortlessMath.com

ISBN: 978-1-63719-039-5

Published by: **Effortless Math Education Inc.**

For Online Math Practice Visit www.EffortlessMath.com

Welcome to
FTCE General Knowledge Math 2022

Thank you for choosing Effortless Math for your FTCE General Knowledge Math test preparation and congratulations on making the decision to take the FTCE General Knowledge test! It's a remarkable move you are taking, one that shouldn't be diminished in any capacity. That's why you need to use every tool possible to ensure you succeed on the test with the highest possible score, and this extensive study guide is one such tool.

If math has never been a strong subject for you, don't worry! This book will help you prepare for (and even ACE) the FTCE General Knowledge test's math section. As test day draws nearer, effective preparation becomes increasingly more important. Thankfully, you have this comprehensive study guide to help you get ready for the test. With this guide, you can feel confident that you will be more than ready for the FTCE General Knowledge Math test when the time comes.

First and foremost, it is important to note that this book is a study guide and not a textbook. It is best read from cover to cover. Every lesson of this "self-guided math book" was carefully developed to ensure that you are making the most effective use of your time while preparing for the test. This up-to-date guide reflects the 2022 test guidelines and will put you on the right track to hone your math skills, overcome exam anxiety, and boost your confidence, so that you can have your best to succeed on the FTCE General Knowledge Math test.

This study guide will:

☑ Explain the format of the FTCE General Knowledge Math test.

☑ Describe specific test-taking strategies that you can use on the test.

☑ Provide FTCE General Knowledge Math test-taking tips.

☑ Review all FTCE General Knowledge Math concepts and topics you will be tested on.

☑ Help you identify the areas in which you need to concentrate your study time.

☑ Offer exercises that help you develop the basic math skills you will learn in each section.

☑ Give **2 realistic and full-length practice tests** (featuring new question types) with detailed answers to help you measure your exam readiness and build confidence.

This resource contains everything you will ever need to succeed on the FTCE General Knowledge Math test. You'll get in-depth instructions on every math topic as well as tips and techniques on how to answer each question type. You'll also get plenty of practice questions to boost your test-taking confidence.

In addition, in the following pages you'll find:

➢ **How to Use This Book Effectively** – This section provides you with step-by-step instructions on how to get the most out of this comprehensive study guide.

➢ **How to study for the FTCE General Knowlege Math Test** – A six-step study program has been developed to help you make the best use of this book and prepare for your FTCE General Knowledge Math test. Here you'll find tips and strategies to guide your study program and help you understand FTCE General Knowledge Math and how to ace the test.

➤ **FTCE General Knowledge Math Review** – Learn everything you need to know about the FTCE General Knowledge Math test.

➤ **FTCE General Knowledge Math Test-Taking Strategies** – Learn how to effectively put these recommended test-taking techniques into use for improving your FTCE General Knowledge Math score.

➤ **Test Day Tips** – Review these tips to make sure you will do your best when the big day comes.

Effortless Math's FTCE General Knowledge Online Center

Effortless Math Online FTCE General Knowledge Center offers a complete study program, including the following:

✓ Step-by-step instructions on how to prepare for the FTCE General Knowledge Math test

✓ Numerous FTCE General Knowledge Math worksheets to help you measure your math skills

✓ Complete list of FTCE General Knowledge Math formulas

✓ Video lessons for all FTCE General Knowledge Math topics

✓ Full-length FTCE General Knowledge Math practice tests

✓ And much more...

No Registration Required.

Visit **EffortlessMath.com/FTCE** to find your online FTCE General Knowledge Math resources.

How to Use This Book Effectively

Look no further when you need a study guide to improve your math skills to succeed on the math portion of the FTCE General Knowledge test. Each chapter of this comprehensive guide to the FTCE General Knowledge Math will provide you with the knowledge, tools, and understanding needed for every topic covered on the test.

It's imperative that you understand each topic before moving onto another one, as that's the way to guarantee your success. Each chapter provides you with examples and a step-by-step guide of every concept to better understand the content that will be on the test. To get the best possible results from this book:

➢ **Begin studying long before your test date**. This provides you ample time to learn the different math concepts. The earlier you begin studying for the test, the sharper your skills will be. Do not procrastinate! Provide yourself with plenty of time to learn the concepts and feel comfortable that you understand them when your test date arrives.

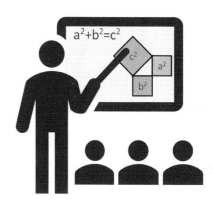

➢ **Practice consistently**. Study FTCE General Knowledge Math concepts at least 20 to 30 minutes a day. Remember, slow and steady wins the race, which can be applied to preparing for the FTCE General Knowledge Math test. Instead of cramming to tackle everything at once, be patient and learn the math topics in short bursts.

➢ Whenever you get a math problem wrong, **mark it off, and review it later** to make sure you understand the concept.

➢ Start each session by **looking over the previous material.**

➢ Once you've reviewed the book's lessons, **take a practice test at the back of the book** to gauge your level of readiness. Then, review your results. Read detailed answers and solutions for each question you missed.

➢ **Take another practice test** to get an idea of how ready you are to take the actual exam. Taking the practice tests will give you the confidence you need on test day. Simulate the FTCE General Knowledge testing environment by sitting in a quiet room free from distraction. Make sure to clock yourself with a timer.

How to Study for the FTCE General Knowledge Math Test

S tudying for the FTCE General Knowledge Math test can be a really daunting and boring task. What's the best way to go about it? Is there a certain study method that works better than others? Well, studying for the FTCE General Knowledge Math can be done effectively. The following six-step program has been designed to make preparing for the FTCE General Knowledge Math test more efficient and less overwhelming.

Step 1 - Create a study plan
Step 2 - Choose your study resources
Step 3 - Review, Learn, Practice
Step 4 - Learn and practice test-taking strategies
Step 5 - Learn the FTCE General Knowledge Test format and take practice tests
Step 6 - Analyze your performance

STEP 1: Create a Study Plan

It's always easier to get things done when you have a plan. Creating a study plan for the FTCE General Knowledge Math test can help you to stay on track with your studies. It's important to sit down and prepare a study plan with what works with your life, work, and any other obligations you may have. Devote enough time each day to studying. It's also a great idea to break down each section of the exam into blocks and study one concept at a time.

It's important to understand that there is no "right" way to create a study plan. Your study plan will be personalized based on your specific needs and learning style.

Follow these guidelines to create an effective study plan for your FTCE General Knowledge Math test:

★ **Analyze your learning style and study habits** – Everyone has a different learning style. It is essential to embrace your individuality and the unique way you learn. Think about what works and what doesn't work for you. Do you prefer FTCE General Knowledge Math prep books or a combination of textbooks and video lessons? Does it work better for you if you study every night for thirty minutes or is it more effective to study in the morning before going to work?

★ **Evaluate your schedule** – Review your current schedule and find out how much time you can consistently devote to FTCE General Knowledge Math study.

★ **Develop a schedule** – Now it's time to add your study schedule to your calendar like any other obligation. Schedule time for study, practice, and review. Plan out which topic you will study on which day to ensure that you're devoting enough time to each concept. Develop a study plan that is mindful, realistic, and flexible.

★ **Stick to your schedule** – A study plan is only effective when it is followed consistently. You should try to develop a study plan that you can follow for the length of your study program.

★ **Evaluate your study plan and adjust as needed** – Sometimes you need to adjust your plan when you have new commitments. Check in with yourself regularly to make sure that you're not falling behind in your study plan. Remember, the most important thing is sticking to your plan. Your study plan is all about helping you be more productive. If you find that your study plan is not as effective as you want, don't get discouraged. It's okay to make changes as you figure out what works best for you.

STEP 2: Choose Your Study Resources

There are numerous textbooks and online resources available for the FTCE General Knowledge Math test, and it may not be clear where to begin. Don't worry! This study guide provides everything you need to fully prepare for your FTCE General Knowledge Math test. In addition to the book content, you can also use Effortless Math's online resources. (video lessons, worksheets,

formulas, etc.) On each page, there is a link (and a QR code) to an online webpage which provides a comprehensive review of the topic, step-by-step instruction, video tutorial, and numerous examples and exercises to help you fully understand the concept.

You can also visit <u>EffortlessMath.com/FTCE</u> to find your online FTCE General Knowledge Math resources.

STEP 3: Review, Learn, Practice

This FTCE General Knowledge Math study guide breaks down each subject into specific skills or content areas. For instance, the percent concept is separated into different topics– percent calculation, percent increase and decrease, percent problems, etc. Use this study guide and Effortless Math online FTCE General Knowledge center to help you go over all key math concepts and topics on the FTCE General Knowledge Math test.

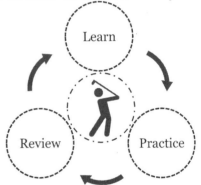

As you read each topic, take notes or highlight the concepts you would like to go over again in the future. If you're unfamiliar with a topic or something is difficult for you, use the link (or the QR code) at the bottom of the page to find the webpage that provides more instruction about that topic. For each math topic, plenty of instructions, step-by-step guides, and examples are provided to ensure you get a good grasp of the material.

Quickly review the topics you do understand to get a brush-up of the material. Be sure to do the practice questions provided at the end of every chapter to measure your understanding of the concepts.

STEP 4: Learn and Practice Test-taking Strategies

In the following sections, you will find important test-taking strategies and tips that can help you earn extra points. You'll learn how to think strategically and when to guess if you don't know the answer to a question. Using FTCE General Knowledge Math test-taking strategies and tips can help you raise your score and do well on the test. Apply test taking strategies on the practice tests to help you boost your confidence.

STEP 5: Learn the FTCE General Knowledge Test Format and Take Practice Tests

The *FTCE General Knowledge Test Review* section provides information about the structure of the FTCE General Knowledge test. Read this section to learn more about the FTCE General Knowledge test structure, different test sections, the number of questions in each section, and the section time limits. When you have a prior understanding of the test format and different types of FTCE General Knowledge Math questions, you'll feel more confident when you take the actual exam.

Once you have read through the instructions and lessons and feel like you are ready to go – take advantage of both of the full-length FTCE General Knowledge Math practice tests available in this study guide. Use the practice tests to sharpen your skills and build confidence.

The FTCE General Knowledge Math practice tests offered at the end of the book are formatted similarly to the actual FTCE General Knowledge Math test. When you take each practice test, try to simulate actual testing conditions. To take the practice tests, sit in a quiet space, time yourself, and work through as many of the questions as time allows. The practice tests are followed by detailed answer explanations to help you find your weak areas, learn from your mistakes, and raise your FTCE General Knowledge Math score.

STEP 6: Analyze Your Performance

After taking the practice tests, look over the answer keys and explanations to learn which questions you answered correctly and which you did not. Never be discouraged if you make a few mistakes. See them as a learning opportunity. This will highlight your strengths and weaknesses.

You can use the results to determine if you need additional practice or if you are ready to take the actual FTCE General Knowledge Math test.

Looking for more?

Visit EffortlessMath.com/FTCE to find hundreds of FTCE General Knowledge Math worksheets, video tutorials, practice tests, FTCE General Knowledge Math formulas, and much more.

Or scan this QR code.

No Registration Required.

FTCE General Knowledge Test Review

Since 1980, Florida teacher certification candidates have been required to pass the FTCE (Florida Teacher Certification Examinations) General Knowledge test. The test is designed to assess the skills and knowledge all teachers and school administrators candidates to begin effective careers as professional educators.

The General Knowledge Test consists of four subtests:

- Essay Subtest (825)
- English Language Skills (ELS) Subtest (826)
- Reading Subtest (827)
- Mathematics Subtest (828)

The Mathematics section of FTCE contains 45 multiple-choice questions assess content in the following areas:

- Number Sense and Operations
- Patterns, Relationships, And Algebra
- Data, Statistics, And Probability
- Geometry and Measurement

A basic calculator is allowed in the mathematics section of FTCE. Test takers have 100 minutes to take the FTCE Mathematics subtest.

In this book, there are 2 complete FTCE Math Tests. Take these tests to see what score you'll be able to receive on a real FTCE.

FTCE General Knowledge Math Test-Taking Strategies

Here are some test-taking strategies that you can use to maximize your performance and results on the FTCE General Knowledge Math test.

#1: USE THIS APPROACH TO ANSWER EVERY FTCE GENERAL KNOWLEDGE MATH QUESTION

- Review the question to identify keywords and important information.

- Translate the keywords into math operations so you can solve the problem.

- Review the answer choices. What are the differences between answer choices?

- Draw or label a diagram if needed.

- Try to find patterns.

- Find the right method to answer the question. Use straightforward math, plug in numbers, or test the answer choices (backsolving).

- Double-check your work.

#2: USE EDUCATED GUESSING

This approach is applicable to the problems you understand to some degree but cannot solve using straightforward math. In such cases, try to filter out as many answer choices as possible before picking an answer. In cases where you don't have a clue about what a certain problem entails, don't waste any time trying to eliminate answer choices. Just choose one randomly before moving onto the next question.

As you can ascertain, direct solutions are the most optimal approach. Carefully read through the question, determine what the solution is using the math you have learned before, then coordinate the answer with one of the choices available to you. Are you stumped? Make your best guess, then move on.

Don't leave any fields empty! Even if you're unable to work out a problem, strive to answer it. Take a guess if you have to. You will not lose points by getting an answer wrong, though you may gain a point by getting it correct!

#3 : BALLPARK

A ballpark answer is a rough approximation. When we become overwhelmed by calculations and figures, we end up making silly mistakes. A decimal that is moved by one unit can change an answer from right to wrong, regardless of the number of steps that you went through to get it. That's where ballparking can play a big part.

If you think you know what the correct answer may be (even if it's just a ballpark answer), you'll usually have the ability to eliminate a couple of choices. While answer choices are usually based on the average student error and/or values that are closely tied, you will still be able to weed out choices that are way far afield. Try to find answers that aren't in the proverbial ballpark when you're looking for a wrong answer on a multiple-choice question. This is an optimal approach to eliminating answers to a problem.

#4 : BACKSOLVING

All questions on the FTCE General Knowledge Math test will be in multiple-choice format. Many test-takers prefer multiple-choice questions, as at least the answer is right there. You'll have four answers to pick from. You simply need to figure out which one is correct. Usually, the best way to go about doing so is "backsolving."

As mentioned earlier, direct solutions are the most optimal approach to answering a question. Carefully read through a problem, calculate a solution, then correspond the answer with one of the choices displayed in front of you. If you can't calculate a solution, your next best approach involves "backsolving."

When backsolving a problem, contrast one of your answer options against the problem you are asked, then see which of them is most relevant. More often than not, answer choices are listed in ascending or descending order. In such cases, try out the choices B or C. If it's not correct, you can go either down or up from there.

#5 : PLUGGING IN NUMBERS

"Plugging in numbers" is a strategy that can be applied to a wide range of different math problems on the FTCE General Knowledge Math test. This approach is typically used to simplify a challenging question so that it is more understandable. By using the strategy carefully, you can find the answer without too much trouble.

The concept is fairly straightforward–replace unknown variables in a problem with certain values. When selecting a number, consider the following:

- Choose a number that's basic (just not too basic). Generally, you should avoid choosing 1 (or even 0). A decent choice is 2.

- Try not to choose a number that is displayed in the problem.

- Make sure you keep your numbers different if you need to choose at least two of them.

- More often than not, choosing numbers merely lets you filter out some of your answer choices. As such, don't just go with the first choice that gives you the right answer.

- If several answers seem correct, then you'll need to choose another value and try again. This time, though, you'll just need to check choices that haven't been eliminated yet.

- If your question contains fractions, then a potential right answer may involve either an LCD (least common denominator) or an LCD multiple.

- 100 is the number you should choose when you are dealing with problems involving percentages.

FTCE Mathematics – Daytime Tips

After practicing and reviewing all the math concepts you've been taught, and taking some FTCE General Knowledge mathematics practice tests, you'll be prepared for test day. Consider the following tips to be extra-ready come test time.

Before Your Test

What to do the night before:

- **Relax!** One day before your test, study lightly or skip studying altogether. You shouldn't attempt to learn something new, either. There are plenty of reasons why studying the evening before a big test can work against you. Put it this way–a marathoner wouldn't go out for a sprint before the day of a big race. Mental marathoners–such as yourself–should not study for any more than one hour 24 hours before a FTCE General Knowledge test. That's because your brain requires some rest to be at its best. The night before your exam, spend some time with family or friends, or read a book.

- **Avoid bright screens** - You'll have to get some good shuteye the night before your test. Bright screens (such as the ones coming from your laptop, TV, or mobile device) should be avoided altogether. Staring at such a screen will keep your brain up, making it hard to drift asleep at a reasonable hour.

- **Make sure your dinner is healthy** - The meal that you have for dinner should be nutritious. Be sure to drink plenty of water as well. Load up on your complex carbohydrates, much like a marathon runner would do. Pasta, rice, and potatoes are ideal options here, as are vegetables and protein sources.

- **Get your bag ready for test day** - The night prior to your test, pack your bag with your stationery, admissions pass, ID, and any other gear that you need. Keep the bag right by your front door.

- **Make plans to reach the testing site** - Before going to sleep, ensure that you understand precisely how you will arrive at the site of the test. If parking is something you'll have to find first, plan for it. If you're dependent on public transit, then review the schedule. You should also make sure that the train/bus/subway/streetcar you use will be running. Find out about road closures as well. If a parent or friend is accompanying you, ensure that they understand what steps they have to take as well.

The Day of the Test ....

■ **Get up reasonably early, but not too early.**

■ **Have breakfast** - Breakfast improves your concentration, memory, and mood. As such, make sure the breakfast that you eat in the morning is healthy. The last thing you want to be is distracted by a grumbling tummy. If it's not your own stomach making those noises, another test taker close to you might be instead. Prevent discomfort or embarrassment by consuming a healthy breakfast. Bring a snack with you if you think you'll need it.

■ **Follow your daily routine** - Do you watch Good Morning America each morning while getting ready for the day? Don't break your usual habits on the day of the test. Likewise, if coffee isn't something you drink in the morning, then don't take up the habit hours before your test. Routine consistency lets you concentrate on the main objective–doing the best you can on your test.

■ **Wear layers** - Dress yourself up in comfortable layers. You should be ready for any kind of internal temperature. If it gets too warm during the test, take a layer off.

■ **Get there on time** - The last thing you want to do is get to the test site late. Rather, you should be there 45 minutes prior to the start of the test. Upon your arrival, try not to hang out with anybody who is nervous. Any anxious energy they exhibit shouldn't influence you.

■ **Leave the books at home** - No books should be brought to the test site. If you start developing anxiety before the test, books could encourage you to do some last-minute studying, which will only hinder you. Keep the books far away–better yet, leave them at home.

■ **Make your voice heard** - If something is off, speak to a proctor. If medical attention is needed or if you'll require anything, consult the proctor prior to the start of the test. Any doubts you have should be clarified. You should be entering the test site with a state of mind that is completely clear.

■ **Have faith in yourself** - When you feel confident, you will be able to perform at your best. When you are waiting for the test to begin, envision yourself receiving an outstanding result. Try to see yourself as someone who knows all the answers, no matter what the questions are. A lot of athletes tend to use this technique–particularly before a big competition. Your expectations will be reflected by your performance.

During your test

■ **Be calm and breathe deeply** - You need to relax before the test, and some deep breathing will go a long way to help you do that. Be confident and calm. You got this. Everybody feels a little stressed out just before an evaluation of any kind is set to begin. Learn some effective breathing exercises. Spend a minute meditating before the test starts. Filter out any negative thoughts you have. Exhibit confidence when having such thoughts.

■ **Concentrate on the test** - Refrain from comparing yourself to anyone else. You shouldn't be distracted by the people near you or random noise. Concentrate exclusively on the test. If you find yourself irritated by surrounding noises, earplugs can be used to block sounds off close to you. Don't forget–the test is going to last several hours if you're taking more than one subject of the test. Some of that time will be dedicated to brief sections. Concentrate on the specific section you are working on during a particular moment. Do not let your mind wander off to upcoming or previous sections.

■ **Skip challenging questions** - Optimize your time when taking the test. Lingering on a single question for too long will work against you. If you don't know what the answer is to a certain question, use your best guess, and mark the question so you can review it later on. There is no need to spend time attempting to solve something you aren't sure about. That time would be better served handling the questions you can actually answer well. You will not be penalized for getting the wrong answer on a test like this.

■ **Try to answer each question individually** - Focus only on the question you are working on. Use one of the test-taking strategies to solve the problem. If you aren't able to come up with an answer, don't get frustrated. Simply skip that question, then move onto the next one.

■ **Don't forget to breathe!** Whenever you notice your mind wandering, your stress levels boosting, or frustration brewing, take a thirty-second break. Shut your eyes, drop your pencil, breathe deeply, and let your shoulders relax. You will end up being more productive when you allow yourself to relax for a moment.

■ **Optimize your breaks** - When break time comes, use the restroom, have a snack, and reactivate your energy for the subsequent section. Doing some stretches can help stimulate your blood flow.

After your test

■ **Take it easy** - You will need to set some time aside to relax and decompress once the test has concluded. There is no need to stress yourself out about what you could've said, or what you may have done wrong. At this point, there's nothing you can do about it. Your energy and time would be better spent on something that will bring you happiness for the remainder of your day.

■ **Redoing the test** - Did you pass the test? Congratulations! Your hard work paid off!

If you have failed your test, though, don't worry! The test can be retaken. In such cases, you will need to follow the retake policy. You also need to re-register to take the exam again.

Contents

Topic	Simplifying Fractions
Notes	✓ Evenly divide both the top and bottom of the fraction by 2, 3, 5, 7, ... etc. ✓ Continue until you can't go any further.
Example	**Simplify** $\frac{36}{48}$ To simplify $\frac{36}{48}$, find a number that both 36 and 48 are divisible by. Both are divisible by 12. Then: $\frac{36}{48} = \frac{36 \div 12}{48 \div 12} = \frac{3}{4}$

Your Turn!		
	1) $\frac{3}{15} =$	2) $\frac{11}{55} =$
	3) $\frac{12}{48} =$	4) $\frac{11}{99} =$
	5) $\frac{15}{75} =$	6) $\frac{25}{100} =$
	7) $\frac{16}{72} =$	8) $\frac{32}{96} =$
	9) $\frac{15}{65} =$	10) $\frac{48}{92} =$

Find more at

bit.ly/3nOGNko

Topic	Simplifying Fractions – Answers
Notes	✓ Evenly divide both the top and bottom of the fraction by $2, 3, 5, 7, \ldots$ etc. ✓ Continue until you can't go any further.
Example	*Simplify* $\frac{36}{48}$ To simplify $\frac{36}{48}$, find a number that both 36 and 48 are divisible by. Both are divisible by 12. Then: $\frac{36}{48} = \frac{36 \div 12}{48 \div 12} = \frac{3}{4}$

Your Turn!

1) $\frac{3}{15} = \frac{1}{5}$

2) $\frac{11}{55} = \frac{1}{5}$

3) $\frac{12}{48} = \frac{1}{4}$

4) $\frac{11}{99} = \frac{1}{9}$

5) $\frac{15}{75} = \frac{1}{5}$

6) $\frac{25}{100} = \frac{1}{4}$

7) $\frac{16}{72} = \frac{2}{9}$

8) $\frac{32}{96} = \frac{1}{3}$

9) $\frac{15}{65} = \frac{3}{13}$

10) $\frac{48}{92} = \frac{12}{23}$

Find more at

bit.ly/3nOGNko

Topic	**Adding and Subtracting Fractions**
Notes	✓ For "like" fractions (fractions with the same denominator), add or subtract the numerators and write the answer over the common denominator. ✓ Find equivalent fractions with the same denominator before you can add or subtract fractions with different denominators. ✓ Adding and Subtracting with the same denominator: $$\frac{a}{b}+\frac{c}{b}=\frac{a+c}{b}\ ,\frac{a}{b}-\frac{c}{b}=\frac{a-c}{b}$$ ✓ Adding and Subtracting fractions with different denominators: $$\frac{a}{b}+\frac{c}{d}=\frac{ad+bc}{bd},\frac{a}{b}-\frac{c}{d}=\frac{ad-bc}{bd}$$
Example	*Find the sum.* $\frac{3}{5}+\frac{2}{3}=\frac{(3)3+(5)(2)}{5\times3}=\frac{19}{15}$ *Subtract.* $\frac{4}{7}-\frac{3}{7}=\frac{1}{7}$
Your Turn! **Find more at** bit.ly/3nKet2X	1) $\frac{2}{3}+\frac{1}{5}=$ 2) $\frac{8}{7}-\frac{3}{5}=$ 3) $\frac{4}{9}+\frac{5}{8}=$ 4) $\frac{5}{8}-\frac{2}{5}=$ 5) $\frac{2}{5}+\frac{1}{6}=$ 6) $\frac{2}{3}-\frac{1}{4}=$ 7) $\frac{8}{9}+\frac{5}{7}=$ 8) $\frac{6}{7}-\frac{5}{9}=$

Topic	**Adding and Subtracting Fractions - Answers**
Notes	✓ For "like" fractions (fractions with the same denominator), add or subtract the numerators and write the answer over the common denominator. ✓ Find equivalent fractions with the same denominator before you can add or subtract fractions with different denominators. ✓ Adding and Subtracting with the same denominator: $$\frac{a}{b}+\frac{c}{b}=\frac{a+c}{b}, \quad \frac{a}{b}-\frac{c}{b}=\frac{a-c}{b}$$ ✓ Adding and Subtracting fractions with different denominators: $$\frac{a}{b}+\frac{c}{d}=\frac{ad+bc}{bd}, \quad \frac{a}{b}-\frac{c}{d}=\frac{ad-bc}{bd}$$
Example	***Find the sum.*** $\frac{3}{5}+\frac{2}{3}=\frac{(3)3+(5)(2)}{5\times 3}=\frac{19}{15}$ ***Subtract.*** $\frac{4}{7}-\frac{3}{7}=\frac{1}{7}$

Your Turn!

1) $\frac{2}{3}+\frac{1}{5}=\frac{13}{15}$	2) $\frac{8}{7}-\frac{3}{5}=\frac{19}{35}$
3) $\frac{4}{9}+\frac{5}{8}=\frac{77}{72}$	4) $\frac{5}{8}-\frac{2}{5}=\frac{9}{40}$
5) $\frac{2}{5}+\frac{1}{6}=\frac{17}{30}$	6) $\frac{2}{3}-\frac{1}{4}=\frac{5}{12}$
7) $\frac{8}{9}+\frac{5}{7}=\frac{101}{63}$	8) $\frac{6}{7}-\frac{5}{9}=\frac{19}{63}$

Find more at

bit.ly/3nKet2X

Topic	**Multiplying and Dividing Fractions**
Notes	✓ Multiplying fractions: multiply the top numbers and multiply the bottom numbers. ✓ Dividing fractions: Keep, Change, Flip Keep first fraction, change division sign to multiplication, and flip the numerator and denominator of the second fraction. Then, solve!
Examples	*Multiply.* $\frac{2}{5} \times \frac{3}{4} =$ Multiply the top numbers and multiply the bottom numbers. $\frac{2}{5} \times \frac{3}{4} = \frac{2 \times 3}{5 \times 4} = \frac{6}{20}$, simplify: $\frac{6}{20} = \frac{6 \div 2}{20 \div 2} = \frac{3}{10}$ *Divide.* $\frac{2}{5} \div \frac{3}{4} =$ Keep first fraction, change division sign to multiplication, and flip the numerator and denominator of the second fraction. Then: $\frac{2}{5} \div \frac{3}{4} = \frac{2}{5} \times \frac{4}{3} = \frac{2 \times 4}{5 \times 3} = \frac{8}{15}$
Your Turn! **Find more at** bit.ly/3haSiQW	1) $\frac{3}{8} \times \frac{2}{5} =$ 2) $\frac{4}{9} \div \frac{3}{4} =$

1) $\frac{3}{8} \times \frac{2}{5} =$	2) $\frac{4}{9} \div \frac{3}{4} =$
3) $\frac{2}{7} \times \frac{3}{5} =$	4) $\frac{2}{5} \div \frac{7}{12} =$
5) $\frac{1}{7} \times \frac{4}{9} =$	6) $\frac{2}{9} \div \frac{3}{7} =$
7) $\frac{4}{7} \times \frac{3}{8} =$	8) $\frac{1}{6} \div \frac{3}{4} =$

Topic	Multiplying and Dividing Fractions - Answers
Notes	✓ Multiplying fractions: multiply the top numbers and multiply the bottom numbers. ✓ Dividing fractions: Keep, Change, Flip Keep first fraction, change division sign to multiplication, and flip the numerator and denominator of the second fraction. Then, solve!
Examples	*Multiply.* $\frac{2}{5} \times \frac{3}{4} =$ Multiply the top numbers and multiply the bottom numbers. $\frac{2}{5} \times \frac{3}{4} = \frac{2 \times 3}{5 \times 4} = \frac{6}{20}$, simplify: $\frac{6}{20} = \frac{6 \div 2}{20 \div 2} = \frac{3}{10}$ *Divide.* $\frac{2}{5} \div \frac{3}{4} =$ Keep first fraction, change division sign to multiplication, and flip the numerator and denominator of the second fraction. Then: $\frac{2}{5} \div \frac{3}{4} = \frac{2}{5} \times \frac{4}{3} = \frac{2 \times 4}{5 \times 3} = \frac{8}{15}$
Your Turn! **Find more at** bit.ly/3haSiQW	1) $\frac{3}{8} \times \frac{2}{5} = \frac{3}{20}$ 2) $\frac{4}{9} \div \frac{3}{4} = \frac{16}{27}$
	3) $\frac{2}{7} \times \frac{3}{5} = \frac{6}{35}$ 4) $\frac{2}{5} \div \frac{7}{12} = \frac{24}{35}$
	5) $\frac{1}{7} \times \frac{4}{9} = \frac{4}{63}$ 6) $\frac{2}{9} \div \frac{3}{7} = \frac{14}{27}$
	7) $\frac{4}{7} \times \frac{3}{8} = \frac{3}{14}$ 8) $\frac{1}{6} \div \frac{3}{4} = \frac{2}{9}$

Topic	**Adding Mixed Numbers**
Notes	Use the following steps for adding mixed numbers. ✓ Add whole numbers of the mixed numbers. ✓ Add the fractions of each mixed number. ✓ Find the Least Common Denominator (LCD) if necessary. ✓ Add whole numbers and fractions. ✓ Write your answer in lowest terms.
Example	*Add mixed numbers.* $1\frac{1}{2} + 2\frac{2}{3} =$ Rewriting our equation with parts separated, $1 + \frac{1}{2} + 2 + \frac{2}{3}$ Add whole numbers: $1 + 2 = 3$ Add fractions: $\frac{1}{2} + \frac{2}{3} = \frac{3}{6} + \frac{4}{6} = \frac{7}{6} = 1\frac{1}{6}$, Now, combine the whole and fraction parts: $3 + 1 + \frac{1}{6} = 4\frac{1}{6}$
Your Turn! **Find more at** bit.ly/2M4oAB	1) $2\frac{1}{15} + 1\frac{2}{5} =$ 2) $1\frac{3}{10} + 3\frac{1}{5} =$ 3) $1\frac{1}{10} + 2\frac{2}{5} =$ 4) $2\frac{5}{6} + 2\frac{2}{9} =$ 5) $2\frac{2}{7} + 1\frac{2}{21} =$ 6) $1\frac{3}{8} + 3\frac{2}{3} =$ 7) $1\frac{1}{6} + 4\frac{2}{7} =$ 8) $2\frac{1}{6} + 1\frac{2}{5} =$

Topic	Adding Mixed Numbers - Answers
Notes	Use the following steps for adding mixed numbers. ✓ Add whole numbers of the mixed numbers. ✓ Add the fractions of each mixed number. ✓ Find the Least Common Denominator (LCD) if necessary. ✓ Add whole numbers and fractions. ✓ Write your answer in lowest terms.
Example	**Add mixed numbers.** $1\frac{1}{2} + 2\frac{2}{3} =$ Rewriting our equation with parts separated, $1 + \frac{1}{2} + 2 + \frac{2}{3}$ Add whole numbers: $1 + 2 = 3$ Add fractions: $\frac{1}{2} + \frac{2}{3} = \frac{3}{6} + \frac{4}{6} = \frac{7}{6} = 1\frac{1}{6}$ Now, combine the whole and fraction parts: $3 + 1 + \frac{1}{6} = 4\frac{1}{6}$

Your Turn!	1) $2\frac{1}{15} + 1\frac{2}{5} = 3\frac{7}{15}$	2) $1\frac{3}{10} + 3\frac{1}{5} = 4\frac{1}{2}$
	3) $1\frac{1}{10} + 2\frac{2}{5} = 3\frac{1}{2}$	4) $2\frac{5}{6} + 2\frac{2}{9} = 5\frac{1}{18}$
	5) $2\frac{2}{7} + 1\frac{2}{21} = 3\frac{8}{21}$	6) $1\frac{3}{8} + 3\frac{2}{3} = 5\frac{1}{24}$
Find more at bit.ly/2M4oABB	7) $1\frac{1}{6} + 4\frac{2}{7} = 5\frac{19}{42}$	8) $2\frac{1}{6} + 1\frac{2}{5} = 3\frac{17}{30}$

Topic	**Subtracting Mixed Numbers**	
Notes	Use the following steps for subtracting mixed numbers. ✓ Convert mixed numbers into improper fractions. $a\frac{c}{b} = \frac{ab+c}{b}$ ✓ Find equivalent fractions with the same denominator for unlike fractions (fractions with different denominators) ✓ Subtract the second fraction from the first one. ✓ Write your answer in lowest terms and convert it into a mixed number if the answer is an improper fraction.	
Example	***Subtract.*** $5\frac{1}{2} - 2\frac{2}{3} =$ Convert mixed numbers into fractions: $5\frac{1}{2} = \frac{5\times2+1}{2} = \frac{11}{2}$ and $2\frac{2}{3} = \frac{2\times3+2}{3} = \frac{8}{3}$, these two fractions are "unlike" fractions. (they have different denominators). Find equivalent fractions with the same denominator. Use this formula: $\frac{a}{b} - \frac{c}{d} = \frac{ad-bc}{bd}$ $\frac{11}{2} - \frac{8}{3} = \frac{(11)(3)-(2)(8)}{2\times3} = \frac{33-16}{6} = \frac{17}{6}$, the answer is an improper fraction, convert it into a mixed number. $\frac{17}{6} = 2\frac{5}{6}$	
Your Turn!	1) $3\frac{1}{4} - 1\frac{2}{3} =$	2) $4\frac{4}{9} - 1\frac{1}{3} =$
	3) $6\frac{1}{4} - 1\frac{2}{7} =$	4) $8\frac{2}{3} - 1\frac{1}{4} =$
Find more at bit.ly/3aD3KDG	5) $8\frac{3}{4} - 1\frac{3}{8} =$	6) $2\frac{3}{8} - 1\frac{2}{3} =$
	7) $8\frac{3}{5} - 1\frac{2}{25} =$	8) $5\frac{2}{3} - 2\frac{4}{7} =$

Topic	Subtracting Mixed Numbers - Answers
Notes	Use the following steps for subtracting mixed numbers. ✓ Convert mixed numbers into improper fractions. $a\frac{c}{b} = \frac{ab+c}{b}$ ✓ Find equivalent fractions with the same denominator for unlike fractions (fractions with different denominators) ✓ Subtract the second fraction from the first one. ✓ Write your answer in lowest terms and convert it into a mixed number if the answer is an improper fraction.
Example	***Subtract.*** $5\frac{1}{2} - 2\frac{2}{3} =$ Convert mixed numbers into fractions: $5\frac{1}{2} = \frac{5\times2+1}{2} = \frac{11}{2}$ and $2\frac{2}{3} = \frac{2\times3+2}{3} = \frac{8}{3}$, these two fractions are "unlike" fractions. (they have different denominators). Find equivalent fractions with the same denominator. Use this formula: $\frac{a}{b} - \frac{c}{d} = \frac{ad-bc}{bd}$ $\frac{11}{2} - \frac{8}{3} = \frac{(11)(3)-(2)(8)}{2\times3} = \frac{33-16}{6} = \frac{17}{6}$, the answer is an improper fraction, convert it into a mixed number. $\frac{17}{6} = 2\frac{5}{6}$
Your Turn! Find more at bit.ly/3aD3KDG 	1) $3\frac{1}{4} - 1\frac{2}{3} = 1\frac{7}{12}$ 2) $4\frac{4}{9} - 1\frac{1}{3} = 3\frac{1}{9}$ 3) $6\frac{1}{4} - 1\frac{2}{7} = 4\frac{27}{28}$ 4) $8\frac{2}{3} - 1\frac{1}{4} = 7\frac{5}{12}$ 5) $8\frac{3}{4} - 1\frac{3}{8} = 7\frac{3}{8}$ 6) $2\frac{3}{8} - 1\frac{2}{3} = \frac{17}{24}$ 7) $8\frac{3}{5} - 1\frac{2}{25} = 7\frac{13}{25}$ 8) $5\frac{2}{3} - 2\frac{4}{7} = 3\frac{2}{21}$

Topic	**Multiplying Mixed Numbers**
Notes	✓ Convert the mixed numbers into fractions. $a\dfrac{c}{b} = a + \dfrac{c}{b} = \dfrac{ab+c}{b}$ ✓ Multiply fractions and simplify if necessary. $\dfrac{a}{b} \times \dfrac{c}{d} = \dfrac{a \times c}{b \times d}$ ✓ If the answer is an improper fraction (numerator is bigger than denominator), convert it into a mixed number.
Example	*Multiply* $2\dfrac{1}{4} \times 3\dfrac{1}{2}$ Convert mixed numbers into fractions: $2\dfrac{1}{4} = \dfrac{2\times4+1}{4} = \dfrac{9}{4}$ and $3\dfrac{1}{2} = \dfrac{3\times2+1}{2} = \dfrac{7}{2}$ Multiply two fractions: $\dfrac{9}{4} \times \dfrac{7}{2} = \dfrac{9\times7}{4\times2} = \dfrac{63}{8}$ The answer is an improper fraction. Convert it into a mixed number: $$\dfrac{63}{8} = 7\dfrac{7}{8}$$

Your Turn!	1) $3\dfrac{1}{3} \times 4\dfrac{1}{8} =$	2) $5\dfrac{1}{2} \times 2\dfrac{6}{7} =$
	3) $3\dfrac{1}{3} \times 3\dfrac{3}{4} =$	4) $2\dfrac{2}{9} \times 6\dfrac{1}{3} =$
Find more at bit.ly/3aPy7XJ	5) $2\dfrac{2}{7} \times 4\dfrac{3}{5} =$	6) $1\dfrac{4}{7} \times 9\dfrac{1}{2} =$
	7) $3\dfrac{3}{5} \times 4\dfrac{1}{3} =$	8) $5\dfrac{1}{4} \times 1\dfrac{1}{7} =$

Topic	Multiplying Mixed Numbers - Answers
Notes	✓ Convert the mixed numbers into fractions. $a\frac{c}{b} = a + \frac{c}{b} = \frac{ab+c}{b}$ ✓ Multiply fractions and simplify if necessary. $\frac{a}{b} \times \frac{c}{d} = \frac{a \times c}{b \times d}$ ✓ If the answer is an improper fraction (numerator is bigger than denominator), convert it into a mixed number.
Example	*Multiply* $2\frac{1}{4} \times 3\frac{1}{2}$ Convert mixed numbers into fractions: $2\frac{1}{4} = \frac{2 \times 4 + 1}{4} = \frac{9}{4}$ and $3\frac{1}{2} = \frac{3 \times 2 + 1}{2} = \frac{7}{2}$ Multiply two fractions: $\frac{9}{4} \times \frac{7}{2} = \frac{9 \times 7}{4 \times 2} = \frac{63}{8}$ The answer is an improper fraction. Convert it into a mixed number: $$\frac{63}{8} = 7\frac{7}{8}$$

Your Turn!		
	1) $3\frac{1}{3} \times 4\frac{1}{8} = 13\frac{3}{4}$	2) $5\frac{1}{2} \times 2\frac{6}{7} = 15\frac{5}{7}$
	3) $3\frac{1}{3} \times 3\frac{3}{4} = 12\frac{1}{2}$	4) $2\frac{2}{9} \times 6\frac{1}{3} = 14\frac{2}{27}$
	5) $2\frac{2}{7} \times 4\frac{3}{5} = 10\frac{18}{35}$	6) $1\frac{4}{7} \times 9\frac{1}{2} = 14\frac{13}{14}$
	7) $3\frac{3}{5} \times 4\frac{1}{3} = 15\frac{3}{5}$	8) $5\frac{1}{4} \times 1\frac{1}{7} = 6$

Find more at

bit.ly/3aPy7XJ

Topic	Dividing Mixed Numbers
Notes	✓ Convert the mixed numbers into improper fractions. $$a\frac{c}{b} = a + \frac{c}{b} = \frac{ab+c}{b}$$ ✓ Divide fractions and simplify if necessary.
Example	*Solve.* $2\frac{1}{3} \div 1\frac{1}{4} =$ Converting mixed numbers to fractions: $2\frac{1}{3} \div 1\frac{1}{4} = \frac{7}{3} \div \frac{5}{4}$ Keep, Change, Flip: $\frac{7}{3} \div \frac{5}{4} = \frac{7}{3} \times \frac{4}{5} = \frac{7\times4}{3\times5} = \frac{28}{15} = 1\frac{13}{15}$
Your Turn!	1) $2\frac{4}{7} \div 1\frac{1}{5} =$

1) $2\frac{4}{7} \div 1\frac{1}{5} =$	2) $3\frac{3}{10} \div 2\frac{5}{8} =$
3) $4\frac{2}{3} \div 3\frac{2}{5} =$	4) $5\frac{4}{5} \div 4\frac{3}{4} =$
5) $1\frac{8}{9} \div 2\frac{3}{7} =$	6) $3\frac{3}{8} \div 2\frac{2}{5} =$
7) $4\frac{1}{5} \div 3\frac{1}{9} =$	8) $4\frac{2}{3} \div 1\frac{8}{9} =$
9) $4\frac{1}{6} \div 3\frac{2}{3} =$	10) $6\frac{1}{3} \div 4\frac{1}{6} =$

Find more at

bit.ly/2KLPk9k

Topic	Dividing Mixed Numbers- Answers
Notes	✓ Convert the mixed numbers into improper fractions. $$a\frac{c}{b} = a + \frac{c}{b} = \frac{ab + c}{b}$$ ✓ Divide fractions and simplify if necessary.
Example	**Solve.** $2\frac{1}{3} \div 1\frac{1}{4} =$ Converting mixed numbers to fractions: $2\frac{1}{3} \div 1\frac{1}{4} = \frac{7}{3} \div \frac{5}{4}$ Keep, Change, Flip: $\frac{7}{3} \div \frac{5}{4} = \frac{7}{3} \times \frac{4}{5} = \frac{7\times4}{3\times5} = \frac{28}{15} = 1\frac{13}{15}$

Your Turn!		
	1) $2\frac{4}{7} \div 1\frac{1}{5} = 2\frac{1}{7}$	2) $3\frac{3}{10} \div 2\frac{5}{8} = 1\frac{9}{35}$
	3) $4\frac{2}{3} \div 3\frac{2}{5} = 1\frac{19}{51}$	4) $5\frac{4}{5} \div 4\frac{3}{4} = 1\frac{21}{95}$
	5) $1\frac{8}{9} \div 2\frac{3}{7} = \frac{7}{9}$	6) $3\frac{3}{8} \div 2\frac{2}{5} = 1\frac{13}{32}$
Find more at bit.ly/2KLPk9k	7) $4\frac{1}{5} \div 3\frac{1}{9} = 1\frac{7}{20}$	8) $4\frac{2}{3} \div 1\frac{8}{9} = 2\frac{8}{17}$
	9) $4\frac{1}{6} \div 3\frac{2}{3} = 1\frac{3}{22}$	10) $6\frac{1}{3} \div 4\frac{1}{6} = 1\frac{13}{25}$

Topic	**Comparing Decimals**
Notes	Decimals: is a fraction written in a special form. For example, instead of writing $\frac{1}{2}$ you can write 0.5. For comparing decimals: ✓ Compare each digit of two decimals in the same place value. ✓ Start from left. Compare hundreds, tens, ones, tenth, hundredth, etc. ✓ To compare numbers, use these symbols: - Equal to $=$, Less than $<$, Greater than $>$ Greater than or equal $\geq$, Less than or equal $\leq$
Examples	*Compare* 0.40 *and* 0.04. 0.40 *is greater than* 0.04, because the tenth place of 0.40 is 4, but the tenth place of 0.04 is zero. Then: $0.40 > 0.04$ *Compare* 0.0912 *and* 0.912. 0.912 *is greater than* 0.0912, because the tenth place of 0.912 is 9, but the tenth place of 0.0912 is zero. Then: $0.0912 < 0.912$

Your Turn!	1) $0.32 \ \square \ 0.36$	2) $1.68 \ \square \ 1.70$
	3) $19.1 \ \square \ 19.09$	4) $2.45 \ \square \ 2.089$
	5) $1.258 \ \square \ 12.58$	6) $0.89 \ \square \ 0.890$
Find more at bit.ly/2WHt2Za	7) $2.657 \ \square \ 3.568$	8) $0.368 \ \square \ 0.683$

Topic	Comparing Decimals – Answers
Notes	Decimals: is a fraction written in a special form. For example, instead of writing $\frac{1}{2}$ you can write 0.5. For comparing decimals: ✓ Compare each digit of two decimals in the same place value. ✓ Start from left. Compare hundreds, tens, ones, tenth, hundredth, etc. ✓ To compare numbers, use these symbols: - Equal to =,　　　　　　　　Less than <,　　Greater than > 　Greater than or equal ≥,　　Less than or equal ≤
Examples	*Compare* 0.40 *and* 0.04. 0.40 *is greater than* 0.04, because the tenth place of 0.40 is 4, but the tenth place of 0.04 is zero. Then: $0.40 > 0.04$ *Compare* 0.0912 *and* 0.912. 0.912 *is greater than* 0.0912, because the tenth place of 0.912 is 9, but the tenth place of 0.0912 is zero. Then: $0.0912 < 0.912$

Your Turn!	1) $0.32 < 0.36$	2) $1.68 < 1.70$
	3) $19.1 > 19.09$	4) $2.45 > 2.089$
	5) $1.258 < 12.58$	6) $0.89 = 0.890$
Find more at bit.ly/2WHt2Za 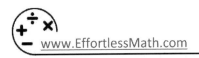	7) $2.657 < 3.568$	8) $0.368 < 0.683$

Topic	**Rounding Decimals**
Notes	✓ We can round decimals to a certain accuracy or number of decimal places. ✓ Let's review place values: For example: 35.4817 3: tens 5: ones 4: tenths 8: hundredths 1: thousandths 7:tens thousandths ✓ To round a decimal, find the place value you'll round to. ✓ Find the digit to the right of the place value you're rounding to. If it is 5 or bigger, add 1 to the place value you're rounding to and remove all digits on its right side. If the digit to the right of the place value is less than 5, keep the place value and remove all digits on the right.
Example	***Round 12.8365 to the hundredth place value.*** First look at the next place value to the right, (thousandths). It's 6 and it is greater than 5. Thus add 1 to the digit in the hundredth place. It is 3. → 3 + 1 = 4, then, the answer is 12.84
Your Turn! **Find more at** bit.ly/3mKEluf	***Round each number to the underlined place value.*** 1) 23.5_6_3= 2) 1.2_2_3= 3) 55._4_23 = 4) 2_5_.62 = 5) 11._2_65 = 6) 33.5_0_5 = 7) 4.4_8_3= 8) 9.0_1_8=

Topic	**Rounding Decimals – Answers**
Notes	✓ We can round decimals to a certain accuracy or number of decimal places. ✓ Let's review place values: For example: $$35.4817$$ 3: tens 5: ones 4: tenths 8: hundredths 1: thousandths 7: tens thousandths ✓ To round a decimal, find the place value you'll round to. ✓ Find the digit to the right of the place value you're rounding to. If it is 5 or bigger, add 1 to the place value you're rounding to and remove all digits on its right side. If the digit to the right of the place value is less than 5, keep the place value and remove all digits on the right.
Example	**Round** 12.8365 **to the hundredth place value.** First look at the next place value to the right, (thousandths). It's 6 and it is greater than 5. Thus add 1 to the digit in the hundredth place. It is 3. $\rightarrow 3 + 1 = 4$, then, the answer is 12.84
Your Turn!	**Round each number to the underlined place value.**

1) 23.5<u>6</u>3 = 23.56	2) 1.2<u>2</u>3 = 1.22
3) 55.<u>4</u>23 = 55.4	4) 2<u>5</u>.62 = 26
5) 11.<u>2</u>65 = 11.3	6) 33.5<u>0</u>5 = 33.51
7) 4.4<u>8</u>3 = 4.48	8) 9.0<u>1</u>8 = 9.02

Find more at

bit.ly/3mKEluf

Topic	Adding and Subtracting Decimals
Notes	✓ Line up the numbers. ✓ Add zeros to have same number of digits for both numbers if necessary. ✓ Add or subtract using column addition or subtraction.
Examples	***Add.*** $2.6 + 5.33 =$ First line up the numbers: $\begin{array}{r} 2.6 \\ +\,5.33 \\ \hline \end{array}$ →Add zeros to have same number of digits for both numbers. $\begin{array}{r} 2.60 \\ +\,5.33 \\ \hline \end{array}$ → Start with the hundredths place. $0 + 3 = 3,$ $\begin{array}{r} 2.60 \\ +\,5.33 \\ \hline 3 \end{array}$ → Continue with tenths place. $6 + 3 = 9,$ $\begin{array}{r} 2.60 \\ +\,5.33 \\ \hline .93 \end{array}$ → Add the ones place. $2 + 5 = 7,$ $\begin{array}{r} 2.60 \\ +\,5.33 \\ \hline 7.93 \end{array}$ ***Subtract.*** $4.79 - 3.13 =$ $\begin{array}{r} 4.79 \\ -\,3.13 \\ \hline \end{array}$ Start with the hundredths place. $9 - 3 = 6,$ $\begin{array}{r} 4.79 \\ -\,3.13 \\ \hline 6 \end{array}$, continue with tenths place. $7 - 1 = 6,$ $\begin{array}{r} 4.79 \\ -\,3.13 \\ \hline .66 \end{array}$, subtract the ones place. $4 - 3 = 1,$ $\begin{array}{r} 4.79 \\ -\,3.13 \\ \hline 1.66 \end{array}$
Your Turn! **Find more at** bit.ly/38uyUdx	1) $28.15 + 16.58 =$ 2) $65.36 - 56.16 =$ 3) $38.19 + 24.18 =$ 4) $57.26 - 43.54 =$ 5) $21.67 + 37.91 =$ 6) $39.58 - 26.44 =$

Topic	Adding and Subtracting Decimals - Answers
Notes	✓ Line up the numbers. ✓ Add zeros to have same number of digits for both numbers if necessary. ✓ Add or subtract using column addition or subtraction.
Examples	***Add.*** $2.6 + 5.33 =$ First line up the numbers: $\begin{array}{r} 2.6 \\ + 5.33 \\ \hline \end{array}$ →Add zeros to have same number of digits for both numbers. $\begin{array}{r} 2.60 \\ + 5.33 \\ \hline \end{array}$ → Start with the hundredths place. $0 + 3 = 3$, $\begin{array}{r} 2.60 \\ + 5.33 \\ \hline 3 \end{array}$ → Continue with tenths place. $6 + 3 = 9$, $\begin{array}{r} 2.60 \\ + 5.33 \\ \hline .93 \end{array}$ → Add the ones place. $2 + 5 = 7$, $\begin{array}{r} 2.60 \\ + 5.33 \\ \hline 7.93 \end{array}$ ***Subtract.*** $4.79 - 3.13 =$ $\begin{array}{r} 4.79 \\ - 3.13 \\ \hline \end{array}$ Start with the hundredths place. $9 - 3 = 6$, $\begin{array}{r} 4.79 \\ - 3.13 \\ \hline 6 \end{array}$, continue with tenths place. $7 - 1 = 6$, $\begin{array}{r} 4.79 \\ - 3.13 \\ \hline .66 \end{array}$, subtract the ones place. $4 - 3 = 1$, $\begin{array}{r} 4.79 \\ - 3.13 \\ \hline 1.66 \end{array}$
Your Turn! **Find more at** bit.ly/38uyUdx	1) $28.15 + 16.58 = 44.73$ 2) $65.36 - 56.16 = 9.20$ 3) $38.19 + 24.18 = 62.37$ 4) $57.26 - 43.54 = 13.72$ 5) $21.67 + 37.91 = 59.58$ 6) $39.58 - 26.44 = 13.14$

Topic	**Multiplying and Dividing Decimals**
Notes	For Multiplication: ✓ Ignore the decimal point and set up and multiply the numbers as you do with whole numbers. ✓ Count the total number of decimal places in both factors. ✓ Place the decimal point in the product. For Division: ✓ If the divisor is not a whole number, move decimal point to right to make it a whole number. Do the same for dividend. ✓ Divide similar to whole numbers.
Examples	***Find the product.*** $1.2 \times 2.3 =$ Set up and multiply the numbers as you do with whole numbers. Line up the numbers: $\frac{\times 23}{}$ → Multiply: $\frac{\times 23}{276}$ → Count the total number of decimal places in both of the factors. There are two decimal digits. Then: $1.2 \times 2.3 = 2.76$ ***Find the quotient.*** $5.6 \div 0.8 =$ The divisor is not a whole number. Multiply it by 10 to get 8. → $0.8 \times 10 = 8$ Do the same for the dividend to get 56 → $5.6 \times 10 = 56$ Now, divide: $56 \div 8 = 7$. The answer is 7.

Your Turn!	1) $1.16 \times 0.5 =$	2) $45.5 \div 5 =$
	3) $0.9 \times 0.68 =$	4) $66.8 \div 0.2 =$
Find more at bit.ly/34DZ0cS	5) $0.16 \times 0.4 =$	6) $58.9 \div 100 =$

Topic	Multiplying and Dividing Decimals – Answers
Notes	For Multiplication: ✓ Ignore the decimal point and set up and multiply the numbers as you do with whole numbers. ✓ Count the total number of decimal places in both factors. ✓ Place the decimal point in the product. For Division: ✓ If the divisor is not a whole number, move decimal point to right to make it a whole number. Do the same for dividend. ✓ Divide similar to whole numbers.
Examples	*Find the product*. $1.2 \times 2.3 =$ Set up and multiply the numbers as you do with whole numbers. Line up the numbers: $\frac{12}{\times 23}$ → Multiply: $\frac{\overset{12}{\times 23}}{276}$ → Count the total number of decimal places in both of the factors. There are two decimal digits. Then: $1.2 \times 2.3 = 2.76$ *Find the quotient*. $5.6 \div 0.8 =$ The divisor is not a whole number. Multiply it by 10 to get 8. → $0.8 \times 10 = 8$ Do the same for the dividend to get 56 → $5.6 \times 10 = 56$ Now, divide: $56 \div 8 = 7$. The answer is 7.

Your Turn! **Find more at** bit.ly/34DZ0cS [QR code]	1) $1.16 \times 0.5 = 0.58$	2) $45.5 \div 5 = 9.1$
	3) $0.9 \times 0.68 = 0.612$	4) $66.8 \div 0.2 = 334$
	5) $0.16 \times 0.4 = 0.064$	6) $58.9 \div 100 = 0.589$

Topic	**Adding and Subtracting Integers**	
Notes	✓ Integers include: zero, counting numbers, and the negative of the counting numbers. $\{\ldots, -3, -2, -1, 0, 1, 2, 3, \ldots\}$ ✓ Add a positive integer by moving to the right on the number line. ✓ Add a negative integer by moving to the left on the number line. Subtract an integer by adding its opposite.	
Examples	*Solve.* $(4) - (-8) =$ Keep the first number and convert the sign of the second number to its opposite. (change subtraction into addition. Then: $(4) + 8 = 12$ *Solve.* $42 + (12 - 26) =$ First subtract the numbers in brackets, $12 - 26 = -14$ Then: $42 + (-14) = \ \rightarrow$ change addition into subtraction: $42 - 14 = 28$	
Your Turn! **Find more at** bit.ly/3aKx5vl	1) $-(13) + 10 =$	2) $(-6) + (-11) + 15 =$
	3) $(-13) + 7 =$	4) $3 - (-7) + 14 =$
	5) $(-7) + (-8) =$	6) $16 - (-4 + 8) =$
	7) $2 + (-6) + 8 =$	8) $-(19) - (-6) + 3 =$

Topic	Adding and Subtracting Integers – Answers
Notes	✓ Integers include: zero, counting numbers, and the negative of the counting numbers. $\{\dots, -3, -2, -1, 0, 1, 2, 3, \dots\}$ ✓ Add a positive integer by moving to the right on the number line. ✓ Add a negative integer by moving to the left on the number line. Subtract an integer by adding its opposite.
Examples	**Solve.** $(4) - (-8) =$ Keep the first number and convert the sign of the second number to its opposite. (change subtraction into addition. Then: $(4) + 8 = 12$ **Solve.** $42 + (12 - 26) =$ First subtract the numbers in brackets, $12 - 26 = -14$ Then: $42 + (-14) = \rightarrow$ change addition into subtraction: $42 - 14 = 28$

Your Turn!	1) $-(13) + 10 = -3$	2) $(-6) + (-11) + 15 = -2$
	3) $(-13) + 7 = -6$	4) $3 - (-7) + 14 = 24$
Find more at bit.ly/3aKx5vl	5) $(-7) + (-8) = -15$	6) $16 - (-4 + 8) = 12$
	7) $2 + (-6) + 8 = 4$	8) $-(19) - (-6) + 3 = -10$

Topic	**Multiplying and Dividing Integers**
Notes	Use following rules for multiplying and dividing integers: ✓ (negative) × (negative) = positive ✓ (negative) ÷ (negative) = positive ✓ (negative) × (positive) = negative ✓ (negative) ÷ (positive) = negative ✓ (positive) × (positive) = positive ✓ (positive) ÷ (negative) = negative
Examples	*Solve.* $2 \times (14 - 17) =$ First subtract the numbers in brackets, $14 - 17 = -3 \rightarrow (2) \times (-3) =$ Now use this rule: (positive) × (negative) = negative $(2) \times (-3) = -6$ *Solve.* $(-7) + (-36 \div 4) =$ First divide -36 by 4, the numbers in brackets, using this rule: (negative) ÷ (positive) = negative Then: $-36 \div 4 = -9$. Now, add -7 and -9: $(-7) + (-9) = -7 - 9 = -16$

Your Turn!	1) $(-4) \times 3 =$	2) $(-48) \div (-8) =$
	3) $(-11) \times (-3) =$	4) $81 \div (-9) =$
	5) $(15 - 12) \times (-7) =$	6) $(-12) \div (3) =$
Find more at bit.ly/3pjQW98	7) $3 \times (-7) =$	8) $(9) \div (-3) =$

Topic	**Multiplying and Dividing Integers - Answers**
Notes	Use following rules for multiplying and dividing integers: ✓ (negative) × (negative) = positive ✓ (negative) ÷ (negative) = positive ✓ (negative) × (positive) = negative ✓ (negative) ÷ (positive) = negative ✓ (positive) × (positive) = positive ✓ (positive) ÷ (negative) = negative
Examples	**Solve.** $2 \times (14 - 17) =$ First subtract the numbers in brackets, $14 - 17 = -3 \to (2) \times (-3) =$ Now use this rule: (positive) × (negative) = negative $(2) \times (-3) = -6$ **Solve.** $(-7) + (-36 \div 4) =$ First divide -36 by 4, the numbers in brackets, using this rule: (negative) ÷ (positive) = negative Then: $-36 \div 4 = -9$. Now, add -7 and -9: $(-7) + (-9) = -7 - 9 = -16$

Your Turn!

1) $(-4) \times 3 = -12$	2) $(-48) \div (-8) = 6$
3) $(-11) \times (-3) = 33$	4) $81 \div (-9) = -9$
5) $(15 - 12) \times (-7) =$ -21	6) $(-12) \div (3) = -4$
7) $3 \times (-7) = -21$	8) $(9) \div (-3) = -3$

Find more at
bit.ly/3pjQW98

Topic	Order of Operation
Notes	When there is more than one math operation, use PEMDAS: (to memorize this rule, remember the phrase "Please Excuse My Dear Aunt Sally") ✓ Parentheses ✓ Exponents ✓ Multiplication and Division (from left to right) ✓ Addition and Subtraction (from left to right)
Examples	***Calculate.*** $(18 - 26) \div (2^4 \div 4) =$ First simplify inside parentheses: $(-8) \div (16 \div 4) = (-8) \div (4)$ Then: $(-8) \div (4) = -2$ ***Solve.*** $(-5 \times 7) - (18 - 3^2) =$ First calculate within parentheses: $(-5 \times 7) - (18 - 3^2) = (-35) - (18 - 9)$ Then: $(-35) - (18 - 9) = -35 - 9 = -44$

Your Turn!		
	1) $(12 \times 3) \div (6 + 6) =$	2) $(36 \div 4) + (11 - 4) =$
	3) $(-9) + (5 \times 6) + 14 =$	4) $(-10 \times 5) \div (2^2 + 1) =$
	5) $[-16(32 \div 2^3)] \div 8 =$	6) $(-7) + (72 \div 3^2) + 12 =$
	7) $[10(64 \div 2^4)] - 3^2 =$	8) $3^3 + (-6 \times 2^3) + 4 =$

Find more at

bit.ly/37LBw7X

Topic	Order of Operation – Answers
Notes	When there is more than one math operation, use PEMDAS: (to memorize this rule, remember the phrase "Please Excuse My Dear Aunt Sally") ✓ Parentheses ✓ Exponents ✓ Multiplication and Division (from left to right) ✓ Addition and Subtraction (from left to right)
Examples	*Calculate.* $(18 - 26) \div (2^4 \div 4) =$ First simplify inside parentheses: $(-8) \div (16 \div 4) = (-8) \div (4)$ Then: $(-8) \div (4) = -2$ *Solve.* $(-5 \times 7) - (18 - 3^2) =$ First calculate within parentheses: $(-5 \times 7) - (18 - 3^2) = (-35) - (18 - 9)$ Then: $(-35) - (18 - 9) = -35 - 9 = -44$

Your Turn!		
	1) $(12 \times 3) \div (6 + 6) = 3$	2) $(36 \div 4) + (11 - 4) = 16$
	3) $(-9) + (5 \times 6) + 14 = 35$	4) $(-10 \times 5) \div (2^2 + 1) = -10$
Find more at bit.ly/37LBw7X	5) $[-16(32 \div 2^3)] \div 8 = -8$	6) $(-7) + (72 \div 3^2) + 12 = 13$
	7) $[10(64 \div 2^4)] - 3^2 =$ 31	8) $3^3 + (-6 \times 2^3) + 4 = -17$

Topic	Integers and Absolute Value
Notes	✓ The absolute value of a number is its distance from zero, in either direction, on the number line. For example, the distance of 9 and -9 from zero on number line is 9. ✓ Absolute value is symbolized by vertical bars, as in $\|x\|$.
Example	*Calculate.* $\|8-5\| \times \|12-16\| =$ First calculate $\|8-5\|$, $\rightarrow \|8-5\| = \|3\|$, the absolute value of 3 is 3, $\|3\| = 3$ $8 \times \|12-16\| =$ Now calculate $\|12-16\|$, $\rightarrow \|12-16\| = \|-4\|$, the absolute value of -4 is 4, $\|-4\| = 4$. Then: $3 \times 4 = 12$

Your Turn!		
	1) $12 - \|6-15\| =$	2) $12 - \|14-18\| - \|6\| =$
	3) $\|21\| - \dfrac{\|-25\|}{5} =$	4) $\|30\| + \dfrac{\|-49\|}{7} =$
	5) $\dfrac{\|7 \times -8\|}{4} \times \dfrac{\|-12\|}{2} =$	6) $\dfrac{\|10 \times -6\|}{5} \times \|-9\| =$
Find more at bit.ly/3aD521u	7) $\dfrac{\|-45\|}{9} \times \dfrac{\|-42\|}{7} =$	8) $\|-25+4\| \times \dfrac{\|-8 \times 3\|}{6} =$

Topic	Integers and Absolute Value – Answers
Notes	✓ The absolute value of a number is its distance from zero, in either direction, on the number line. For example, the distance of 9 and -9 from zero on number line is 9. ✓ Absolute value is symbolized by vertical bars, as in $\lvert x \rvert$.
Example	***Calculate.*** $\lvert 8 - 5 \rvert \times \lvert 12 - 16 \rvert =$ First calculate $\lvert 8 - 5 \rvert$, $\rightarrow \lvert 8 - 5 \rvert = \lvert 3 \rvert$, the absolute value of 3 is 3, $\lvert 3 \rvert = 3$ $8 \times \lvert 12 - 16 \rvert =$ Now calculate $\lvert 12 - 16 \rvert$, $\rightarrow \lvert 12 - 16 \rvert = \lvert -4 \rvert$, the absolute value of -4 is 4, $\lvert -4 \rvert = 4$. Then: $3 \times 4 = 12$

Your Turn!		
	1) $12 - \lvert 6 - 15 \rvert = 3$	2) $12 - \lvert 14 - 18 \rvert - \lvert 6 \rvert = 2$
	3) $\lvert 21 \rvert - \dfrac{\lvert -25 \rvert}{5} = 16$	4) $\lvert 30 \rvert + \dfrac{\lvert -49 \rvert}{7} = 37$
Find more at bit.ly/3aD521u	5) $\dfrac{\lvert 7 \times -8 \rvert}{4} \times \dfrac{\lvert -12 \rvert}{2} = 84$	6) $\dfrac{\lvert 10 \times -6 \rvert}{5} \times \lvert -9 \rvert = 108$
	7) $\dfrac{\lvert -45 \rvert}{9} \times \dfrac{\lvert -42 \rvert}{7} = 30$	8) $\lvert -25 + 4 \rvert \times \dfrac{\lvert -8 \times 3 \rvert}{6} = 84$

Topic	**Simplifying Ratios**
Notes	✓ Ratios are used to make comparisons between two numbers. ✓ Ratios can be written as a fraction, using the word "to", or with a colon. ✓ You can calculate equivalent ratios by multiplying or dividing both sides of the ratio by the same number.
Examples	*Simplify.* $18:63 =$ Both numbers 18 and 63 are divisible by $9 \Rightarrow 18 \div 9 = 2, 63 \div 9 = 7,$ Then: $18:63 = 2:7$ *Simplify.* $\frac{25}{45} =$ Both numbers 25 and 45 are divisible by 5, $\Rightarrow 25 \div 5 = 5, 45 \div 5 = 9,$ Then: $\frac{25}{45} = \frac{5}{9}$

Your Turn!	1) $\frac{6}{48} = -$	2) $\frac{35}{60} = -$
	3) $\frac{15}{35} = -$	4) $\frac{42}{54} = -$
	5) $\frac{12}{36} = -$	6) $\frac{30}{80} = -$
Find more at bit.ly/3nKwq0Z	7) $\frac{16}{36} = -$	8) $\frac{30}{108} = -$

Topic	Simplifying Ratios – Answers
Notes	✓ Ratios are used to make comparisons between two numbers. ✓ Ratios can be written as a fraction, using the word "to", or with a colon. ✓ You can calculate equivalent ratios by multiplying or dividing both sides of the ratio by the same number.
Examples	***Simplify.*** $18:63 =$ Both numbers 18 and 63 are divisible by 9 $\Rightarrow 18 \div 9 = 2, 63 \div 9 = 7$, Then: $18:63 = 2:7$ ***Simplify.*** $\frac{25}{45} =$ Both numbers 25 and 45 are divisible by 5, $\Rightarrow 25 \div 5 = 5, 45 \div 5 = 9$, Then: $\frac{25}{45} = \frac{5}{9}$

Your Turn!	1) $\frac{6}{48} = \frac{1}{8}$	2) $\frac{35}{60} = \frac{7}{12}$
	3) $\frac{15}{35} = \frac{3}{7}$	4) $\frac{42}{54} = \frac{7}{9}$
	5) $\frac{12}{36} = \frac{1}{3}$	6) $\frac{30}{80} = \frac{3}{8}$
Find more at bit.ly/3nKwq0Z	7) $\frac{16}{36} = \frac{4}{9}$	8) $\frac{30}{108} = \frac{5}{18}$

Topic	**Proportional Ratios**
Notes	✓ Two ratios are proportional if they represent the same relationship. ✓ A proportion means that two ratios are equal. It can be written in two ways: $$\frac{a}{b} = \frac{c}{d} \qquad a:b = c:d$$
Example	**Solve this proportion for** x. $\dfrac{5}{8} = \dfrac{35}{x}$ Use cross multiplication: $\dfrac{5}{8} = \dfrac{35}{x} \Rightarrow 5 \times x = 8 \times 35 \Rightarrow 5x = 280$ Divide to find x: $\quad x = \dfrac{280}{5} \Rightarrow x = 56$

Your Turn!	1) $\dfrac{1}{3} = \dfrac{7}{x} \Rightarrow x = $ _____	2) $\dfrac{4}{3} = \dfrac{20}{x} \Rightarrow x = $ _____
	3) $\dfrac{3}{11} = \dfrac{6}{x} \Rightarrow x = $ _____	4) $\dfrac{12}{20} = \dfrac{x}{200} \Rightarrow x = $ _____
	5) $\dfrac{9}{12} = \dfrac{27}{x} \Rightarrow x = $ _____	6) $\dfrac{14}{16} = \dfrac{x}{80} \Rightarrow x = $ _____
Find more at bit.ly/37GHQxp	7) $\dfrac{5}{14} = \dfrac{40}{x} \Rightarrow x = $ _____	8) $\dfrac{8}{12} = \dfrac{36}{x} \Rightarrow x = $ _____

Topic	**Proportional Ratios - Answers**
Notes	✓ Two ratios are proportional if they represent the same relationship. ✓ A proportion means that two ratios are equal. It can be written in two ways: $$\frac{a}{b} = \frac{c}{d} \qquad a:b = c:d$$
Example	*Solve this proportion for x.* $\frac{5}{8} = \frac{35}{x}$ Use cross multiplication: $\frac{5}{8} = \frac{35}{x} \Rightarrow 5 \times x = 8 \times 35 \Rightarrow 5x = 280$ Divide to find x: $x = \frac{280}{5} \Rightarrow x = 56$

Your Turn!		
	1) $\frac{1}{3} = \frac{7}{x} \Rightarrow x = 21$	2) $\frac{4}{3} = \frac{20}{x} \Rightarrow x = 15$
	3) $\frac{3}{11} = \frac{6}{x} \Rightarrow x = 22$	4) $\frac{12}{20} = \frac{x}{200} \Rightarrow x = 120$
	5) $\frac{9}{12} = \frac{27}{x} \Rightarrow x = 36$	6) $\frac{14}{16} = \frac{x}{80} \Rightarrow x = 70$
Find more at bit.ly/37GHQxp	7) $\frac{5}{14} = \frac{40}{x} \Rightarrow x = 112$	8) $\frac{8}{12} = \frac{36}{x} \Rightarrow x = 54$

Topic	**Create Proportion**
Notes	✓ To create a proportion, simply find (or create) two equal fractions. ✓ Use cross products to solve proportions or to test whether two ratios are equal and form a proportion. $\frac{a}{b} = \frac{c}{d} \Rightarrow a \times d = c \times b$
Example	***State if this pair of ratios form a proportion.*** $\frac{2}{3}$ *and* $\frac{12}{30}$ Use cross multiplication: $\frac{2}{3} = \frac{12}{30} \rightarrow 2 \times 30 = 12 \times 3 \rightarrow 60 = 36$, which is not correct. Therefore, this pair of ratios doesn't form a proportion.

Your Turn!

State if each pair of ratios form a proportion.

1) $\frac{3}{5}$ *and* $\frac{24}{45}$

2) $\frac{4}{9}$ *and* $\frac{16}{24}$

3) $\frac{3}{11}$ *and* $\frac{9}{33}$

4) $\frac{7}{10}$ *and* $\frac{14}{20}$

5) $\frac{7}{9}$ *and* $\frac{48}{81}$

6) $\frac{6}{8}$ *and* $\frac{12}{14}$

7) $\frac{2}{10}$ *and* $\frac{6}{30}$

8) $\frac{3}{18}$ *and* $\frac{19}{28}$

Find more at

bit.ly/37GHQxp

9) Solve.

Five pencils costs \$0.50. How many pencils can you buy for \$2.50? _____

Topic	Create Proportion – Answers
Notes	✓ To create a proportion, simply find (or create) two equal fractions. ✓ Use cross products to solve proportions or to test whether two ratios are equal and form a proportion. $\frac{a}{b} = \frac{c}{d} \Rightarrow a \times d = c \times b$
Example	***State if this pair of ratios form a proportion.*** $\frac{2}{3}$ *and* $\frac{12}{30}$ Use cross multiplication: $\frac{2}{3} = \frac{12}{30} \rightarrow 2 \times 30 = 12 \times 3 \rightarrow 60 = 36$, which is not correct. Therefore, this pair of ratios doesn't form a proportion.
Your Turn!	***State if each pair of ratios form a proportion.***

1) $\frac{3}{5}$ and $\frac{24}{45}$, *No*	2) $\frac{4}{9}$ and $\frac{16}{24}$, *No*
3) $\frac{3}{11}$ and $\frac{9}{33}$, *Yes*	4) $\frac{7}{10}$ and $\frac{14}{20}$, *Yes*
5) $\frac{7}{9}$ and $\frac{48}{81}$, *No*	6) $\frac{6}{8}$ and $\frac{12}{14}$, *No*
7) $\frac{2}{10}$ and $\frac{6}{30}$, *Yes*	8) $\frac{3}{18}$ and $\frac{19}{28}$, *No*

Find more at

bit.ly/37GHQxp

9) Solve.

Five pencils costs $0.50. How many pencils can you buy for $2.50? **5 pencils**

Topic	**Similarity and Ratios**
Notes	✓ Two figures are similar if they have the same shape. ✓ Two or more figures are similar if the corresponding angles are equal, and the corresponding sides are in proportion.
Example	*Following triangles are similar. What is the value of unknown side?* **Solution:** Find the corresponding sides and write a proportion: $\frac{4}{12} = \frac{x}{9}$. Now, use cross product to solve for x: $\frac{4}{12} = \frac{x}{9} \rightarrow 4 \times 9 = 12 \times x \rightarrow 36 = 12x$. Divide both sides by 12. Then: $12x = 36 \rightarrow \frac{36}{12} = \frac{12x}{12} \rightarrow x = 3$. The missing side is 3.

Your Turn!

1)

2)

3)

4)

5)

6)

Topic	Similarity and Ratios - Answers
Notes	✓ Two figures are similar if they have the same shape. ✓ Two or more figures are similar if the corresponding angles are equal, and the corresponding sides are in proportion.
Example	*Following triangles are similar. What is the value of unknown side?* **Solution:** Find the corresponding sides and write a proportion: $\frac{4}{12} = \frac{x}{9}$. Now, use cross product to solve for x: $\frac{4}{12} = \frac{x}{9} \rightarrow 4 \times 9 = 12 \times x \rightarrow 36 = 12x$. Divide both sides by 12. Then: $12x = 36 \rightarrow \frac{36}{12} = \frac{12x}{12} \rightarrow x = 3$. The missing side is 3.

Your Turn!	
1) 10	2) 11
3) 4	4) 8
5) 10	6) 9

Find more at

bit.ly/2KKKmcV

Topic	Percent Problems

Notes	✓ In each percent problem, we are looking for the base, or part or the percent.
	✓ Use the following equations to find each missing section.
	   ○ Base = Part ÷ Percent
	   ○ Part = Percent × Base
	   ○ Percent = Part ÷ Base

Examples	**18 *is what percent of* 30?** In this problem, we are looking for the percent. Use the following equation: $Percent = Part \div Base \rightarrow Percent = 18 \div 30 = 0.6 = 60\%$ **40 *is* 20% *of what number?*** Use the following formula: $Base = Part \div Percent \rightarrow Base = 40 \div 0.20 = 200$ 40 is 20% of 200.
Your Turn! **Find more at** bit.ly/34Gy3FL	1) What is 20 percent of 500? 2) 24 is what percent of 160? 3) 60 is 5 percent of what number? 4) 48 is what percent of 300? 5) 84 is 28 percent of what number? 6) 63 is what percent of 700? 7) 63 is 21 percent of what number? 8) 42 is what percent of 600?

Topic	Percent Problems – Answers

Notes	✓ In each percent problem, we are looking for the base, or part or the percent.
	✓ Use the following equations to find each missing section.
	  ○ Base = Part ÷ Percent
	  ○ Part = Percent × Base
	  ○ Percent = Part ÷ Base

Examples	**18 *is what percent of* 30?** In this problem, we are looking for the percent. Use the following equation: $Percent = Part \div Base \rightarrow Percent = 18 \div 30 = 0.6 = 60\%$ **40 *is* 20% *of what number?*** Use the following formula: $Base = Part \div Percent \rightarrow Base = 40 \div 0.20 = 200$ 40 is 20% of 200.

Your Turn!		
Your Turn!	1) What is 20 percent of 500? 100	2) 24 is what percent of 160? 15%
	3) 60 is 5 percent of what number? 1,200	4) 48 is what percent of 300? 16%
	5) 84 is 28 percent of what number? 300	6) 63 is what percent of 700? 9%
Find more at bit.ly/34Gy3FL 	7) 63 is 21 percent of what number? 300	8) 42 is what percent of 600? 7%

Topic	**Percent of Increase and Decrease**
Notes	✓ Percent of change (increase or decrease) is a mathematical concept that represents the degree of change over time. ✓ To find the percentage of increase or decrease: 1- New Number – Original Number 2- The result ÷ Original Number × 100 Or use this formula: Percent of change = $\frac{new\ number\ -\ original\ number}{original\ number} \times 100$
Example	The price of a printer increases from \$40 to \$50. What is the percent increase? **Solution:** Percent of change = $\frac{new\ number\ -\ original\ number}{original\ number} \times 100 =$ $\frac{50\ -\ 40}{40} \times 100 = 25$ The percentage increase is 25. It means that the price of the printer increased 25%.
Your Turn! **Find more at** bit.ly/3pgPQes	1) In a class, the number of students has been increased from 30 to 33. What is the percentage increase? _____ % 2) The price of gasoline rose from \$4.60 to \$4.83 in one month. By what percent did the gas price rise? _____ % 3) A shirt was originally priced at \$60.00. It went on sale for \$54.00. What was the percent that the shirt was discounted? _____ % 4) Jason got a raise, and his hourly wage increased from \$40 to \$56. What is the percent increase? _____ %

Topic	Percent of Increase and Decrease – Answers
Notes	✓ Percent of change (increase or decrease) is a mathematical concept that represents the degree of change over time. ✓ To find the percentage of increase or decrease: 1- New Number – Original Number 2- The result ÷ Original Number × 100 Or use this formula: Percent of change = $\frac{new\ number\ -\ original\ number}{original\ number} \times 100$
Example	The price of a printer increases from \$40 to \$50. What is the percent increase? **Solution:** Percent of change = $\frac{new\ number\ -\ original\ number}{original\ number} \times 100 = \frac{50-40}{40} \times 100 =$ 25 The percentage increase is 25. It means that the price of the printer increased 25%.
Your Turn!	1) In a class, the number of students has been increased from 30 to 33. What is the percentage increase? 10%
	2) The price of gasoline rose from \$4.60 to \$4.83 in one month. By what percent did the gas price rise? 5%
Find more at bit.ly/3pgPQes	3) A shirt was originally priced at \$60.00. It went on sale for \$54.00. What was the percent that the shirt was discounted? --10%
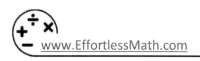	4) Jason got a raise, and his hourly wage increased from \$40 to \$56. What is the percent increase? 40%

Topic	Discount, Tax and Tip
Notes	✓ Discount = Multiply the regular price by the rate of discount ✓ Selling price = original price – discount ✓ To find tax, multiply the tax rate to the taxable amount (income, property value, etc.) ✓ To find tip, multiply the rate to the selling price.
Example	The original price of a table is $300 and the tax rate is 6%. What is the final price of the table? **Solution:** First find the tax amount. To find tax: Multiply the tax rate to the taxable amount. Tax rate is 6% or 0.06. Then: $0.06 \times 300 = 18$. The tax amount is $18. Final price is: $300 + $18 = $318

Your Turn!	1) Original price of a chair: $350 Tax: 12%, Selling price: _____	2) Original price of a computer: $600 Discount: 15%, Selling price: _____
	3) Original price of a printer: $250 Tax: 10%, Selling price: _____	4) Original price of a sofa: $620 Discount: 25%, Selling price: _____
	5) Original price of a mattress: $800 Tax: 12%, Selling price: _____	6) Original price of a book: $150 Discount: 60%, Selling price: _____
Find more at bit.ly/2Je5lo0	7) Restaurant bill: $24.00 Tip: 25%, Final amount: _____	8) Restaurant bill: $80.00 Tip: 15%, Final amount: _____

Topic	Discount, Tax and Tip – Answers
Notes	✓ Discount = Multiply the regular price by the rate of discount ✓ Selling price = original price – discount ✓ To find tax, multiply the tax rate to the taxable amount (income, property value, etc.) ✓ To find tip, multiply the rate to the selling price.
Example	*The original price of a table is $300 and the tax rate is 6%. What is the final price of the table?* **Solution:** First find the tax amount. To find tax: Multiply the tax rate to the taxable amount. Tax rate is 6% or 0.06. Then: $0.06 \times 300 = 18$. The tax amount is $18. Final price is: $300 + $18 = $318

Your Turn!		
Find more at bit.ly/2Je5lo0 	1) Original price of a chair: $350 Tax: 12%, Selling price: $392	2) Original price of a computer: $ 600 Discount: 15%, Selling price: $510
	3) Original price of a printer: $250 Tax: 10%, Selling price: $275	4) Original price of a sofa: $620 Discount: 25%, Selling price: $465
	5) Original price of a mattress: $800 Tax: 12%, Selling price: $896	6) Original price of a book: $150 Discount: 60%, Selling price: $60
	7) Restaurant bill: $24.00 Tip: 25%, Final amount: $30	8) Restaurant bill: $80.00 Tip: 15%, Final amount: $92

Topic	Simple Interest
Notes	✓ Simple Interest: The charge for borrowing money or the return for lending it. To solve a simple interest problem, use this formula: Interest = principal x rate x time $\Rightarrow$ $I = p \times r \times t$
Example	***Find simple interest for*** $3,000$ ***investment at*** 5% ***for 4 years.*** **Solution:** Use Interest formula: $I = prt$ ($P = \$3,000$, r $= 5\% = 0.05$ and $t = 4$) Then: $I = 3,000 \times 0.05 \times 4 = \$600$

Your Turn!		
Find more at bit.ly/3nJli3D	1) $200 at 3% for 2 years. Simple interest: $_____	2) $4,200 at 4% for 5 years. Simple interest: $_____
	3) $720 at 2% for 5 years. Simple interest: $_____	4) $2,200 at 8% for 4 years. Simple interest: $_____
	5) $1,800 at 3% for 2 years. Simple interest: $_____	6) $530 at 4% for 5 years. Simple interest: $_____
	7) $5,100 at 6% for 6 months. Simple interest: $_____	8) $960 at 5% for 3 months. Simple interest: $_____

Topic	Simple Interest – Answers
Notes	✓ Simple Interest: The charge for borrowing money or the return for lending it. To solve a simple interest problem, use this formula: Interest = principal x rate x time $\Rightarrow$ $I = p \times r \times t$

Example	**Find simple interest for** $3,000$ **investment at** 5% **for 4 years**.
	   Solution: Use Interest formula: $I = prt$ ($P = \$3,000$, r $= 5\% = 0.05$ and $t = 4$)
	   Then: $I = 3,000 \times 0.05 \times 4 = \$600$

Your Turn!		
	1) $200 at 3% for 2 years. Simple interest: $12	2) $4,200 at 4% for 5 years. Simple interest: $840
	3) $720 at 2% for 5 years. Simple interest: $72	4) $2,200 at 8% for 4 years. Simple interest: $704
	5) $1,800 at 3% for 2 years. Simple interest: $108	6) $530 at 4% for 5 years. Simple interest: $106
Find more at bit.ly/3nJli3D	7) $5,100 at 6% for 6 months. Simple interest: $153	8) $960 at 5% for 3 months. Simple interest: $12

Topic	Simplifying Variable Expressions
Notes	✓ In algebra, a variable is a letter used to stand for a number. The most common letters are: $x, y, z, a, b, c, m, and\ n$. ✓ Algebraic expression is an expression contains integers, variables, and the math operations such as addition, subtraction, multiplication, division, etc. ✓ In an expression, we can combine "like" terms. (values with same variable and same power)
Example	*Simplify this expression*. $(6x + 8x + 9) =?$ Combine like terms. Then: $(6x + 8x + 9) = 14x + 9$ **(remember you cannot combine variables and numbers).**

Your Turn!	1) $6x + 4 - 7x =$	2) $5 + 3x + 2x =$
	3) $8x + 3 - 3x =$	4) $-2 - x^2 - 6x^2 =$
	5) $3 + 10x^2 + 2 =$	6) $8x^2 + 6x + 7x^2 =$
	7) $5x^2 - 12x^2 + 8x =$	8) $2x^2 - 2x - x + 5x^2 =$
Find more at bit.ly/2WFVudQ	9) $6x - (10 - 25x) =$	10) $16x - (60x - 50) =$

Topic	Simplifying Variable Expressions – Answers
Notes	✓ In algebra, a variable is a letter used to stand for a number. The most common letters are: $x, y, z, a, b, c, m, and\ n$. ✓ Algebraic expression is an expression contains integers, variables, and the math operations such as addition, subtraction, multiplication, division, etc. ✓ In an expression, we can combine "like" terms. (values with same variable and same power)
Example	*Simplify this expression.* $(6x + 8x + 9) = ?$ Combine like terms. Then: $(6x + 8x + 9) = 14x + 9$ *(remember you cannot combine variables and numbers).*

Your Turn!		
	1) $6x + 4 - 7x =$ $\qquad -x + 4$	2) $5 + 3x + 2x =$ $\qquad 5x + 5$
	3) $8x + 3 - 3x =$ $\qquad 5x + 3$	4) $-2 - x^2 - 6x^2 =$ $\qquad -7x^2 - 2$
	5) $3 + 10x^2 + 2 =$ $\qquad 10x^2 + 5$	6) $8x^2 + 6x + 7x^2 =$ $\qquad 15x^2 + 6x$
	7) $5x^2 - 12x^2 + 8x =$ $\qquad -7x^2 + 8x$	8) $2x^2 - 2x - x + 5x^2 =$ $\qquad 7x^2 - 3x$
Find more at bit.ly/2WFVudQ	9) $6x - (10 - 25x) =$ $\qquad 31x - 10$	10) $16x - (60x - 50) =$ $\qquad -44x + 50$

Topic	**Simplifying Polynomial Expressions**
Notes	✓ In mathematics, a polynomial is an expression consisting of variables and coefficients that involves only the operations of addition, subtraction, multiplication, and non–negative integer exponents of variables. $$P(x) = a_n x^n + a_{n-1} x^{n-1} + \dots + a_2 x^2 + a_1 x + z$$
Example	*Simplify this expression.* $(2x^2 - x^4) - (4x^4 - x^2) =$ First use distributive property: → multiply $(-)$ into $(4x^4 - x^2)$ $(2x^2 - x^4) - (4x^4 - x^2) = 2x^2 - x^4 - 4x^4 + x^2$ Then combine "like" terms: $2x^2 - x^4 - 4x^4 + x^2 = 3x^2 - 5x^4$ And write in standard form: $3x^2 - 5x^4 = -5x^4 + 3x^2$

Your Turn!

1) $(x^3 + 3x^2) - (10x + 4x^2) =$	2) $(3x^5 + 5x^3) - (6x^3 + 9x^2) =$
3) $(12x^4 + 4x^2) - (2x^2 - 6x^4) =$	4) $14x - 3x^2 - 2(6x^2 + 6x^3) =$
5) $(5x^3 - 3) + 5(2x^2 - 3x^3) =$	6) $(4x^3 - 2x) - 2(4x^3 - 2x^4) =$
7) $3(3x - 2x^3) - 4(x^3 + 5x^2) =$	8) $(4x^2 - 3x) - (4x^3 + 6x^2) =$

Find more at

bit.ly/2WT5gtn

Topic	**Simplifying Polynomial Expressions – Answers**
Notes	✓ In mathematics, a polynomial is an expression consisting of variables and coefficients that involves only the operations of addition, subtraction, multiplication, and non–negative integer exponents of variables. $$P(x) = a_n x^n + a_{n-1} x^{n-1} + \dots + a_2 x^2 + a_1 x + a_0$$
Example	*Simplify this expression.* $(2x^2 - x^4) - (4x^4 - x^2) =$ First use distributive property: → multiply $(-)$ into $(4x^4 - x^2)$ $(2x^2 - x^4) - (4x^4 - x^2) = 2x^2 - x^4 - 4x^4 + x^2$ Then combine "like" terms: $2x^2 - x^4 - 4x^4 + x^2 = 3x^2 - 5x^4$ And write in standard form: $3x^2 - 5x^4 = -5x^4 + 3x^2$

Your Turn!

1) $(x^3 + 3x^2) - (10x + 4x^2) =$ $x^3 - x^2 - 10x$	2) $(3x^5 + 5x^3) - (6x^3 + 9x^2) =$ $3x^5 - x^3 - 9x^2$
3) $(12x^4 + 4x^2) - (2x^2 - 6x^4) =$ $18x^4 + 2x^2$	4) $14x - 3x^2 - 2(6x^2 + 6x^3) =$ $-12x^3 - 15x^2 + 14x$
5) $(5x^3 - 3) + 5(2x^2 - 3x^3) =$ $-10x^3 + 10x^2 - 3$	6) $(4x^3 - 2x) - 2(4x^3 - 2x^4) =$ $4x^4 - 4x^3 - 2x$
7) $3(3x - 2x^3) - 4(x^3 + 5x^2) =$ $-10x^3 - 20x^2 + 9x$	8) $(4x^2 - 3x) - (4x^3 + 6x^2) =$ $-4x^3 - 2x^2 - 3x$

Find more at

bit.ly/2WT5gtn

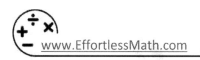

Topic	**Evaluating One Variable**
Notes	✓ To evaluate one variable expression, find the variable and substitute a number for that variable. ✓ Perform the arithmetic operations.
Example	*Find the value of this expression for* $x = -3$. $-3x - 13$ **Solution:** Substitute -3 for x, then: $-3x - 13 = -3(-3) - 13 = 9 - 13 = -4$

Your Turn!		
	1) $x = -2 \Rightarrow 4x + 9 =$ ____	2) $x = 3 \Rightarrow 5(3x + 5) =$ ____
	3) $x = -1 \Rightarrow 6x + 4 =$ ____	4) $x = 7 \Rightarrow 6(5x + 3) =$ ____
	5) $x = 4 \Rightarrow 5(3x + 2) =$ ____	6) $x = 6 \Rightarrow 3(2x + 4) =$ ____
	7) $x = 3 \Rightarrow 7(3x + 1) =$ ____	8) $x = 8 \Rightarrow 3(3x + 7) =$ ____
	9) $x = 8 \Rightarrow 3(x + 6) =$ ____	10) $x = 6 \Rightarrow 3(2x + 3) =$ ____

Find more at

bit.ly/3ppujQZ

Topic	Evaluating One Variable – Answers
Notes	✓ To evaluate one variable expression, find the variable and substitute a number for that variable. ✓ Perform the arithmetic operations.
Example	*Find the value of this expression for* $x = -3$. $\quad -3x - 13$ **Solution:** Substitute -3 for x, then: $-3x - 13 = -3(-3) - 13 = 9 - 13 = -4$

Your Turn!		
	1) $x = -2 \Rightarrow 4x + 9 = 1$	2) $x = 3 \Rightarrow 5(3x + 5) = 70$
	3) $x = -1 \Rightarrow 6x + 4 = -2$	4) $x = 7 \Rightarrow 6(5x + 3) = 228$
	5) $x = 4 \Rightarrow 5(3x + 2) = 70$	6) $x = 6 \Rightarrow 3(2x + 4) = 48$
	7) $x = 3 \Rightarrow 7(3x + 1) = 70$	8) $x = 8 \Rightarrow 3(3x + 7) = 93$
Find more at bit.ly/3ppujQZ	9) $x = 8 \Rightarrow 3(x + 6) = 42$	10) $x = 6 \Rightarrow 3(2x + 3) = 45$

Topic	**Evaluating Two Variables**	
Notes	✓ To evaluate an algebraic expression, substitute a number for each variable. ✓ Perform the arithmetic operations to find the value of the expression.	
Example	***Evaluate this expression for*** $a = 4$ ***and*** $b = -2$. $5a - 6b$ **Solution:** Substitute 4 for a, and -2 for b, then: $$5a - 6b = 5(4) - 6(-2) = 20 + 12 = 32$$	
Your Turn!	1) $-3a + 5b$, $a = 3$, $b = 2$ ————	2) $4x + 2y$, $x = -1$, $y = 4$ ————
	3) $-5a + 3b$, $a = 2$, $b = -2$ ————	4) $3x - 4y$, $x = 6$, $y = 2$ ————
	5) $2z + 14 + 6k$, $z = 5$, $k = 3$ ————	6) $7a - (9 - 3b)$, $a = 1$, $b = 1$ ————
	7) $-6a + 3b$, $a = 4$, $b = 3$ ————	8) $-2a + b$, $a = 6$, $b = 9$ ————
Find more at bit.ly/2JfrzWJ	9) $5x + 3y$, $x = 2$, $y = 9$ ————	10) $z + 7 + 3k$, $z = 4$, $k = 2$ ————

Topic	Evaluating Two Variables – Answers
Notes	✓ To evaluate an algebraic expression, substitute a number for each variable. ✓ Perform the arithmetic operations to find the value of the expression.
Example	*Evaluate this expression for* $a = 4$ *and* $b = -2$. $\;5a - 6b$ **Solution:** Substitute 4 for a, and -2 for b, then: $5a - 6b = 5(4) - 6(-2) = 20 + 12 = 32$

Your Turn!		
	1) $-3a + 5b$, $a = 3$, $b = 2$ $\qquad 1$	2) $4x + 2y$, $x = -1$, $y = 4$ $\qquad 4$
	3) $-5a + 3b$, $a = 2$, $b = -2$ $\qquad -16$	4) $3x - 4y$, $x = 6$, $y = 2$ $\qquad 10$
	5) $2z + 14 + 6k$, $z = 5$, $k = 3$ 42	6) $7a - (9 - 3b)$, $a = 1$, $b = 1$ $\qquad 1$
	7) $-6a + 3b$, $a = 4$, $b = 3$ -15	8) $-2a + b$, $a = 6$, $b = 9$ $\qquad -3$
Find more at bit.ly/2JfrzWJ	9) $5x + 3y$, $x = 2$, $y = 9$ 37	10) $z + 7 + 3k$, $z = 4$, $k = 2$ 17

Topic	The Distributive Property
Notes	✓ The distributive property (or the distributive property of multiplication over addition and subtraction) simplifies and solves expressions in the form of: $a(b + c)$ or $a(b - c)$ ✓ Distributive Property rule: $$a(b + c) = ab + ac$$
Example	**Simply.** $(5)(2x - 8)$ **Solution:** Use Distributive Property rule: $a(b + c) = ab + ac$ $$(5)(2x - 8) = (5 \times 2x) + (5) \times (-8) = 10x - 40$$
Your Turn! **Find more at** bit.ly/38qCaXs	1) $(-3)(2 - 4x) =$ 2) $(3 - 2x)(-5)$ 3) $6(5 - 9x) =$ 4) $10(3 - 5x) =$ 5) $5(6 - 5x) =$ 6) $(-2)(-5x + 3) =$ 7) $(8 - 9x)(5) =$ 8) $(-16x + 15)(-3) =$ 9) $(-6x + 8)(4) =$ 10) $(-12x + 21)(-3) =$

Topic	The Distributive Property – Answers
Notes	✓ The distributive property (or the distributive property of multiplication over addition and subtraction) simplifies and solves expressions in the form of: $a(b + c)$ or $a(b - c)$ ✓ Distributive Property rule: $$a(b + c) = ab + ac$$
Example	***Simply.*** $(5)(2x - 8)$ **Solution:** Use Distributive Property rule: $a(b + c) = ab + ac$ $$(5)(2x - 8) = (5 \times 2x) + (5) \times (-8) = 10x - 40$$

Your Turn!		
	1) $(-3)(2 - 4x) = 12x - 6$	2) $(3 - 2x)(-5) = 10x - 15$
	3) $6(5 - 9x) = -54x + 30$	4) $10(3 - 5x) = -50x + 30$
	5) $5(6 - 5x) = -25x + 30$	6) $(-2)(-5x + 3) = 10x - 6$
	7) $(8 - 9x)(5) = -45x + 40$	8) $(-16x + 15)(-3) =$ $48x - 45$
	9) $(-6x + 8)(4) = -24x + 32$	10)$(-12x + 21)(-3) =$ $36x - 63$

Find more at

bit.ly/38qCaXs

Topic	One–Step Equations

Notes	✓ You only need to perform one Math operation in order to solve the one-step equations.
	
	✓ To solve one-step equation, find the inverse (opposite) operation is being performed.
	
	✓ The inverse operations are:
	
	   - Addition and subtraction
	
	   - Multiplication and division

Example	*Solve this equation.* $x + 42 = 60 \Rightarrow x = ?$ Here, the operation is addition and its inverse operation is subtraction. To solve this equation, subtract 42 from both sides of the *equation:* $x + 42 - 42 = 60 - 42$ Then simplify: $x + 42 - 42 = 60 - 42 \Rightarrow x = 18$

Your Turn!		
	1) $x - 12 = 44 \Rightarrow x =$ ____	2) $15 = 11 + x \Rightarrow x =$ ____
	3) $x - 22 = 54 \Rightarrow x =$ ____	4) $x + 14 = 24 \Rightarrow x =$ ____
	5) $4x = 24 \Rightarrow x =$ ____	6) $\frac{x}{6} = -3 \Rightarrow x =$ ____
Find more at bit.ly/37Jq0tK	7) $66 = 22x \Rightarrow x =$ ____	8) $\frac{x}{18} = 3 \Rightarrow x =$ ____

Topic	One–Step Equations – Answers

Notes	✓ You only need to perform one Math operation in order to solve the one-step equations.
	
	✓ To solve one-step equation, find the inverse (opposite) operation is being performed.
	
	✓ The inverse operations are:
	   - Addition and subtraction
	   - Multiplication and division

Example	*Solve this equation.* $x + 42 = 60 \Rightarrow x = ?$ Here, the operation is addition and its inverse operation is subtraction. To solve this equation, subtract 42 from both sides of the *equation:* $x + 42 - 42 = 60 - 42$ Then simplify: $x + 42 - 42 = 60 - 42 \Rightarrow x = 18$

Your Turn!		
	1) $x - 12 = 44 \Rightarrow x = 56$	2) $15 = 11 + x \Rightarrow x = 4$
	3) $x - 22 = 54 \Rightarrow x = 76$	4) $x + 14 = 24 \Rightarrow x = 10$
	5) $4x = 24 \Rightarrow x = 6$	6) $\frac{x}{6} = -3 \Rightarrow x = -18$
Find more at bit.ly/37Jq0tK	7) $66 = 22x \Rightarrow x = 3$	8) $\frac{x}{18} = 3 \Rightarrow x = 54$

Topic	Multi –Step Equations
Notes	✓ Combine "like" terms on one side. ✓ Bring variables to one side by adding or subtracting. ✓ Simplify using the inverse of addition or subtraction. ✓ Simplify further by using the inverse of multiplication or division. ✓ Check your solution by plugging the value of the variable into the original equation.
Example	*Solve this equation for* x. $2x - 3 = 13$ **Solution:** The inverse of subtraction is addition. Add 3 to both sides of the equation. Then: $2x - 3 = 13 \Rightarrow 2x - 3 = 13 + 3$ $\Rightarrow 2x = 16$. Now, divide both sides by 2, then: $\frac{2x}{2} = \frac{16}{2} \Rightarrow x = 8$ Now, check the solution: $x = 8 \Rightarrow 2x - 3 = 13 \Rightarrow 2(8) - 3 = 13 \Rightarrow 16 - 3 = 13$ The answer $x = 8$ is correct.

Your Turn!		
	1) $5x - 15 = 10 \Rightarrow x =$	2) $14 - 2x = -6 + 2x \Rightarrow x =$
	3) $3(4 - 2x) = 24 \Rightarrow x =$	4) $15 + 5x = -7 - 6x \Rightarrow x =$
Find more at bit.ly/3nQbSEB	5) $-2(5 + x) = 2 \Rightarrow x =$	6) $12 - 2x = -3 - 5x \Rightarrow x =$
	7) $18 = -(x - 8) \Rightarrow x =$	8) $13 - 5x = -5 - 2x \Rightarrow x =$

Topic	Multi –Step Equations – Answers
Notes	✓ Combine "like" terms on one side. ✓ Bring variables to one side by adding or subtracting. ✓ Simplify using the inverse of addition or subtraction. ✓ Simplify further by using the inverse of multiplication or division. ✓ Check your solution by plugging the value of the variable into the original equation.
Example	*Solve this equation for* x. $2x - 3 = 13$ **Solution:** The inverse of subtraction is addition. Add 3 to both sides of the equation. Then: $2x - 3 = 13 \Rightarrow 2x - 3 = 13 + 3$ $\Rightarrow 2x = 16$. Now, divide both sides by 2, then: $\frac{2x}{2} = \frac{16}{2} \Rightarrow x = 8$ Now, check the solution: $x = 8 \Rightarrow 2x - 3 = 13 \Rightarrow 2(8) - 3 = 13 \Rightarrow 16 - 3 = 13$ The answer $x = 8$ is correct.

Your Turn!		
	1) $5x - 15 = 10 \Rightarrow x = 5$	2) $14 - 2x = -6 + 2x \Rightarrow x = 5$
	3) $3(4 - 2x) = 24 \Rightarrow x = -2$	4) $15 + 5x = -7 - 6x \Rightarrow x = -2$
	5) $-2(5 + x) = 2 \Rightarrow x = -6$	6) $12 - 2x = -3 - 5x \Rightarrow x = -5$
	7) $18 = -(x - 8) \Rightarrow x = -10$	8) $13 - 5x = -5 - 2x \Rightarrow x = 6$

Find more at

bit.ly/3nObSFB

Topic	System of Equations
Notes	✓ A system of equations contains two equations and two variables. For example, consider the system of equations: $x - 2y = -2, x + 2y = 10$ ✓ The easiest way to solve a system of equation is using the elimination method. The elimination method uses the addition property of equality. You can add the same value to each side of an equation. ✓ For the first equation above, you can add $x + 2y$ to the left side and 10 to the right side of the first equation: $x - 2y + (x + 2y) = -2 + 10$. Now, if you simplify, you get: $x - 2y + (x + 2y) = -2 + 10 \rightarrow 2x = 8 \rightarrow x = 4$. Now, substitute 4 for the x in the first equation: $4 - 2y = -2$. By solving this equation, $y = 3$
Example	What is the value of x and y in this system of equations? $$\begin{cases} 3x - y = 7 \\ -x + 4y = 5 \end{cases}$$ **Solution:** Solving System of Equations by Elimination: $\begin{array}{r} 3x - y = 7 \\ -x + 4y = 5 \\ \hline \end{array}$ Multiply the second equation by 3, then add it to the first equation. $\begin{array}{r} 3x - y = 7 \\ 3(-x + 4y = 5) \end{array} \Rightarrow \begin{array}{r} 3x - y = 7 \\ -3x + 12y = 15) \end{array} \Rightarrow 11y = 22 \Rightarrow y = 2$. Now, substitute 2 for y in the first equation and solve for x. $3x - (2) = 7 \Rightarrow 3x = 9 \Rightarrow x = 3$
Your Turn! **Find more at** bit.ly/3mPGO6k	1) $-4x + 4y = 8$ $\qquad -4x + 2y = 6$ $x =$ ___ $y =$ ___ 2) $-5x + y = -3$ $\qquad 3x - 8y = 24$ $x =$ ___ $y =$ ___ 3) $y = -2$ $\qquad 4x - 3y = 8$ $x =$ ___ $y =$ ___ 4) $y = -3x + 5$ $\qquad 5x - 4y = -3$ $x =$ ___ $y =$ ___ 5) $20x - 18y = -26$ $\qquad -10x + 6y = 22$ $x =$ ___ $y =$ ___ 6) $-9x - 12y = 15$ $\qquad 2x - 6y = 14$ $x =$ ___ $y =$ ___

Topic	System of Equations- Answers
Notes	✓ A system of equations contains two equations and two variables. For example, consider the system of equations: $x - 2y = -2, x + 2y = 10$ ✓ The easiest way to solve a system of equation is using the elimination method. The elimination method uses the addition property of equality. You can add the same value to each side of an equation. ✓ For the first equation above, you can add $x + 2y$ to the left side and 10 to the right side of the first equation: $x - 2y + (x + 2y) = -2 + 10$. Now, if you simplify, you get: $x - 2y + (x + 2y) = -2 + 10 \rightarrow 2x = 8 \rightarrow x = 4$. Now, substitute 4 for the x in the first equation: $4 - 2y = -2$. By solving this equation, $y = 3$
Example	What is the value of x and y in this system of equations? $\begin{cases} 3x - y = 7 \\ -x + 4y = 5 \end{cases}$ **Solution:** Solving System of Equations by Elimination: $\begin{array}{l} 3x - y = 7 \\ \underline{-x + 4y = 5} \end{array}$ Multiply the second equation by 3, then add it to the first equation. $\begin{array}{l} 3x - y = 7 \\ \underline{3(-x + 4y = 5)} \end{array} \Rightarrow \begin{array}{l} 3x - y = 7 \\ \underline{-3x + 12y = 15)} \end{array} \Rightarrow 11y = 22 \Rightarrow y = 2$. Now, substitute 2 for y in the first equation and solve for x. $3x - (2) = 7 \Rightarrow 3x = 9 \Rightarrow x = 3$
Your Turn! **Find more at** bit.ly/3mPGO6k 	1) $-4x + 4y = 8$ $-4x + 2y = 6$ $x = -1$ $y = 1$ 2) $-5x + y = -3$ $3x - 8y = 24$ $x = 0$ $y = -3$
	3) $y = -2$ $4x - 3y = 8$ $x = \dfrac{1}{2}$ $y = -2$ 4) $y = -3x + 5$ $5x - 4y = -3$ $x = 1$ $y = 2$
	5) $20x - 18y = -26$ $-10x + 6y = 22$ $x = -4$ $y = -3$ 6) $-9x - 12y = 15$ $2x - 6y = 14$ $x = 1$ $y = -2$

Topic	Graphing Single–Variable Inequalities
Notes	✓ An inequality compares two expressions using an inequality sign. ✓ Inequality signs are: "less than" $<$, "greater than" $>$, "less than or equal to" $\leq$, and "greater than or equal to" $\geq$. ✓ To graph a single–variable inequality, find the value of the inequality on the number line. ✓ For less than ($<$) or greater than ($>$) draw open circle on the value of the variable. If there is an equal sign too, then use filled circle. ✓ Draw an arrow to the right for greater or to the left for less than.
Example	***Draw a graph for this inequality.*** $x < 5$ **Solution:** Since, the variable is less than 5, then we need to find 5 in the number line and draw an open circle on it. Then, draw an arrow to the left.
Your Turn! **Find more at** bit.ly/3aJ4GGo	1) $x < 3$ 2) $x \geq -2$ 3) $x \geq -3$ 4) $x \leq 6$ 5) $x > -6$ 6) $2 > x$ 7) $-3 \leq x$ 8) $x > 1$

Topic	Graphing Single–Variable Inequalities- Answers
Notes	✓ An inequality compares two expressions using an inequality sign. ✓ Inequality signs are: "less than" $<$, "greater than" $>$, "less than or equal to" $\leq$, and "greater than or equal to" $\geq$. ✓ To graph a single–variable inequality, find the value of the inequality on the number line. ✓ For less than ($<$) or greater than ($>$) draw open circle on the value of the variable. If there is an equal sign too, then use filled circle. ✓ Draw an arrow to the right for greater or to the left for less than.
Example	***Draw a graph for this inequality.*** $x < 5$ **Solution:** Since, the variable is less than 5, then we need to find 5 in the number line and draw an open circle on it. Then, draw an arrow to the left.

Your Turn!

1) $x < 3$

2) $x \geq -2$

3) $x \geq -3$

4) $x \leq 6$

5) $x > -6$

6) $2 > x$

Find more at

bit.ly/3aJ4GGo

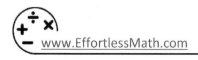

7) $-3 \leq x$

8) $x > 1$

Topic	One–Step Inequalities
Notes	✓ Inequality signs are: "less than" <, "greater than" >, "less than or equal to" ≤, and "greater than or equal to" ≥. ✓ You only need to perform one Math operation in order to solve the one-step inequalities. ✓ To solve one-step inequalities, find the inverse (opposite) operation is being performed. ✓ For dividing or multiplying both sides by negative numbers, flip the direction of the inequality sign.
Example	***Solve this inequality.*** $x + 12 < 60 \Rightarrow$ _____ Here, the operation is addition and its inverse operation is subtraction. To solve this inequality, subtract 12 from both sides of the ***inequality:*** $x + 12 - 12 < 60 - 12$ Then simplify: $x < 48$

Your Turn!		
	1) $3x < -9 \Rightarrow$ _____	2) $x + 5 > 29 \Rightarrow$ _____
	3) $-3x \geq 36 \Rightarrow$ _____	4) $x - 16 \leq 4 \Rightarrow$ _____
	5) $\frac{x}{2} \geq -9 \Rightarrow$ _____	6) $48 < 6x \Rightarrow$ _____
	7) $88 \leq 22x \Rightarrow$ _____	8) $\frac{x}{6} > 8 \Rightarrow$ _____

Find more at

bit.ly/3rrEIgL

Topic	One–Step Inequalities - Answers
Notes	✓ Inequality signs are: "less than" <, "greater than" >, "less than or equal to" ≤, and "greater than or equal to" ≥. ✓ You only need to perform one Math operation in order to solve the one-step inequalities. ✓ To solve one-step inequalities, find the inverse (opposite) operation is being performed. ✓ For dividing or multiplying both sides by negative numbers, flip the direction of the inequality sign.
Example	**Solve this inequality.** $x + 12 < 60 \Rightarrow$ _____ Here, the operation is addition and its inverse operation is subtraction. To solve this inequality, subtract 12 from both sides of the **inequality:** $x + 12 - 12 < 60 - 12$ Then simplify: $x < 48$

Your Turn!		
Find more at bit.ly/3rrElgL	1) $3x < -9 \Rightarrow x < -3$	2) $x + 5 > 29 \Rightarrow x > 24$
	3) $-3x \geq 36 \Rightarrow x \leq -12$	4) $x - 16 \leq 4 \Rightarrow x \leq 20$
	5) $\frac{x}{2} \geq -9 \Rightarrow x \geq -18$	6) $48 < 6x \Rightarrow 8 < x$
	7) $88 \leq 22x \Rightarrow 4 \leq x$	8) $\frac{x}{6} > 8 \Rightarrow x > 48$

Topic	Multi –Step Inequalities
Notes	✓ Isolate the variable. ✓ Simplify using the inverse of addition or subtraction. ✓ Simplify further by using the inverse of multiplication or division. ✓ For dividing or multiplying both sides by negative numbers, flip the direction of the inequality sign.
Example	**Solve this inequality.** $3x + 12 \leq 21$ **Solution:** First subtract 12 from both sides: $3x + 12 - 12 \leq 21 - 12$ Then simplify: $3x + 12 - 12 \leq 21 - 12 \rightarrow 3x \leq 9$ Now divide both sides by 3: $\frac{3x}{3} \leq \frac{9}{3} \rightarrow x \leq 3$

Your Turn!		
	1) $4x + 3 < 39 \rightarrow$ _____	2) $5x - 9 \leq 6 \rightarrow$ _____
	3) $2x - 5 \leq 17 \rightarrow$ _____	4) $14 - 7x \geq -7 \rightarrow$ _____
	5) $18 - 6x \geq -6 \rightarrow$ _____	6) $2x - 18 \leq 16 \rightarrow$ _____
Find more at bit.ly/2WK1xOr	7) $9 + 6x < 45 \rightarrow$ _____	8) $7 - 4x < 19 \rightarrow$ _____

Topic	Multi –Step Inequalities – Answers
Notes	✓ Isolate the variable. ✓ Simplify using the inverse of addition or subtraction. ✓ Simplify further by using the inverse of multiplication or division. ✓ For dividing or multiplying both sides by negative numbers, flip the direction of the inequality sign.
Example	***Solve this inequality*.** $3x + 12 \leq 21$ **Solution:** First subtract 12 from both sides: $3x + 12 - 12 \leq 21 - 12$ Then simplify: $3x + 12 - 12 \leq 21 - 12 \rightarrow 3x \leq 9$ Now divide both sides by 3: $\frac{3x}{3} \leq \frac{9}{3} \rightarrow x \leq 3$

Your Turn!		
	1) $4x + 3 < 39 \rightarrow x < 9$	2) $5x - 9 \leq 6 \rightarrow x \leq 3$
	3) $2x - 5 \leq 17 \rightarrow x \leq 11$	4) $14 - 7x \geq -7 \rightarrow x \leq 3$
	5) $18 - 6x \geq -6 \rightarrow x \leq 4$	6) $2x - 18 \leq 16 \rightarrow x \leq 17$
Find more at bit.ly/2WK1xOr	7) $9 + 6x < 45 \rightarrow x < 6$	8) $7 - 4x < 19 \rightarrow x > -3$

Topic	**Finding Slope**
Notes	✓ The slope of a line represents the direction of a line on the coordinate plane. ✓ A line on coordinate plane can be drawn by connecting two points. ✓ To find the slope of a line, we need two points. ✓ The slope of a line with two points A (x_1, y_1) and B (x_2, y_2) can be found by using this formula: $\frac{y_2 - y_1}{x_2 - x_1} = \frac{rise}{\text{run}}$ ✓ The equation of a line is typically written as $y = mx + b$ where m is the slope and b is the y-intercept.
Examples	*Find the slope of the line through these two points:* $(4, -12)$ *and* $(9, 8)$. **Solution:** Slope $= \frac{y_2 - y_1}{x_2 - x_1}$. Let (x_1, y_1) be $(4, -12)$ and (x_2, y_2) be $(9, 8)$. ***Then:*** slope $= \frac{y_2 - y_1}{x_2 - x_1} = \frac{8 - (-12)}{9 - 4} = \frac{8 + 12}{5} = \frac{20}{5} = 4$ *Find the slope of the line with equation* $y = 5x - 6$ **Solution:** when the equation of a line is written in the form of $y = mx + b$, the slope is m. In this line: $y = 5x - 6$, the slope is 5.

Your Turn!

Find more at

bit.ly/3nMJYJv

1) $(1, 3), (5, 7)$ Slope = ____	2) $(-2, 2), (0, 4)$ Slope = ____
3) $(4, -2), (2, 4)$ Slope = ____	4) $(-4, -1), (0, 7)$ Slope = ____
5) $y = 4x + 15$ Slope = ____	6) $y = -6x + 3$ Slope = ____

Topic	Finding Slope – Answers
Notes	✓ The slope of a line represents the direction of a line on the coordinate plane. ✓ A line on coordinate plane can be drawn by connecting two points. ✓ To find the slope of a line, we need two points. ✓ The slope of a line with two points A (x_1, y_1) and B (x_2, y_2) can be found by using this formula: $\dfrac{y_2 - y_1}{x_2 - x_1} = \dfrac{rise}{run}$ ✓ The equation of a line is typically written as $y = mx + b$ where m is the slope and b is the y-intercept.
Examples	*Find the slope of the line through these two points:* $(4, -12)$ *and* $(9, 8)$. **Solution:** Slope $= \dfrac{y_2 - y_1}{x_2 - x_1}$. Let (x_1, y_1) be $(4, -12)$ and (x_2, y_2) be $(9, 8)$. **Then:** slope $= \dfrac{y_2 - y_1}{x_2 - x_1} = \dfrac{8 - (-12)}{9 - 4} = \dfrac{8 + 12}{5} = \dfrac{20}{5} = 4$ *Find the slope of the line with equation* $y = 5x - 6$ **Solution:** when the equation of a line is written in the form of $y = mx + b$, the slope is m. In this line: $y = 5x - 6$, the slope is 5.
Your Turn! **Find more at** bit.ly/3nMJYJv	1) $(1, 3), (5, 7)$ Slope $= 1$	2) $(-2, 2), (0, 4)$ Slope $= 1$
	3) $(4, -2), (2, 4)$ Slope $= -3$	4) $(-4, -1), (0, 7)$ Slope $= 2$
	5) $y = 4x + 15$ Slope $= 4$	6) $y = 6x + 3$ Slope $= 6$

Topic	**Graphing Lines Using Slope–Intercept Form**
Notes	✓ Slope–intercept form of a line: given the slope m and the y–intercept (the intersection of the line and y-axis) b, then the equation of the line is: $$y = mx + b$$
Example	***Sketch the graph of*** $y = -2x - 1$. **Solution:** To graph this line, we need to find two points. When x is zero the value of y is -1. And when y is zero the value of x is $-\frac{1}{2}$. $$x = 0 \rightarrow y = -2(0) - 1 = -1, y = 0 \rightarrow 0$$ $$= -2x - 1 \rightarrow x = -\frac{1}{2}$$ Now, we have two points: $(0, -1)$ and $(-\frac{1}{2}, 0)$. Find the points and graph the line. Remember that the slope of the line is $-\frac{1}{2}$.
Your Turn! **Find more at** bit.ly/3hfdnJL	1) $y = -4x + 1$ 2) $y = -x - 5$

Topic	Graphing Lines Using Slope–Intercept Form - Answers
Notes	✓ Slope–intercept form of a line: given the slope m and the y–intercept (the intersection of the line and y-axis) b, then the equation of the line is: $$y = mx + b$$
Example	***Sketch the graph of*** $y = -2x - 1$. **Solution:** To graph this line, we need to find two points. When x is zero the value of y is -1. And when y is zero the value of x is $-\frac{1}{2}$. $$x = 0 \rightarrow y = -2(0) - 1 = -1, y = 0 \rightarrow 0$$ $$= -2x - 1 \rightarrow x = -\frac{1}{2}$$ Now, we have two points: $(0, -1)$ and $\left(-\frac{1}{2}, 0\right)$. Find the points and graph the line. Remember that the slope of the line is $-\frac{1}{2}$.
Your Turn! **Find more at** bit.ly/3hfdnJL	1) $y = -4x + 1$ 2) $y = -x - 5$

Topic	**Writing Linear Equations**	
Notes	✓ The equation of a line: $y = mx + b$ ✓ Identify the slope. ✓ Find the y–intercept. This can be done by substituting the slope and the coordinates of a point (x, y) on the line.	
Example	**Write the equation of the line through $(3, 1)$ and $(-1, 5)$.** **Solution:** $Slop = \frac{y_2 - y_1}{x_2 - x_1} = \frac{5 - 1}{-1 - 3} = \frac{4}{-4} = -1 \rightarrow m = -1$ To find the value of b, you can use either points. The answer will be the same: $y = -x + b$ $(3, 1) \rightarrow 1 = -3 + b \rightarrow b = 4$ $(-1, 5) \rightarrow 5 = -(-1) + b \rightarrow b = 4$ The equation of the line is: $y = -x + 4$	
Your Turn! **Find more at** bit.ly/3nMKcAl	1) through: $(-1, 2), (1, 4)$ $y =$	2) through: $(8, 1), (5, 4)$ $y =$
	3) through: $(5, -1), (8, 2)$ $y =$	4) through: $(-2, 4), (4, -8)$ $y =$
	5) through: $(6, -5), (-5, 6)$ $y =$	6) through: $(4, -4), (-2, 8)$ $y =$
	7) through $(-3, 6)$, Slope: 2 $y =$	8) through $(4, 3)$, Slope: -4 $y =$

Topic	Writing Linear Equations – Answers
Notes	✓ The equation of a line: $y = mx + b$ ✓ Identify the slope. ✓ Find the y–intercept. This can be done by substituting the slope and the coordinates of a point (x, y) on the line.
Example	**Write the equation of the line through** $(3, 1)$ **and** $(-1, 5)$. **Solution:** $Slop = \frac{y_2 - y_1}{x_2 - x_1} = \frac{5 - 1}{-1 - 3} = \frac{4}{-4} = -1 \rightarrow m = -1$ To find the value of b, you can use either points. The answer will be the same: $y = -x + b$ $(3, 1) \rightarrow 1 = -3 + b \rightarrow b = 4$ $(-1, 5) \rightarrow 5 = -(-1) + b \rightarrow b = 4$ The equation of the line is: $y = -x + 4$

Your Turn!	1) through: $(-1, 2), (1, 4)$ $y = x + 3$	2) through: $(8, 1), (5, 4)$ $y = -x + 9$
	3) through: $(5, -1), (8, 2)$ $y = x - 6$	4) through: $(-2, 4), (4, -8)$ $y = -2x$
	5) through: $(6, -5), (-5, 6)$ $y = -x + 1$	6) through: $(4, -4), (-2, 8)$ $y = -2x + 4$
Find more at bit.ly/3nMKcAl	7) through $(-3, 6)$, Slope: 2 $y = 2x + 12$	8) through $(4, 3)$, Slope: -4 $y = -4x + 19$

Topic	**Finding Midpoint**
Notes	✓ The middle of a line segment is its midpoint. ✓ The Midpoint of two endpoints A (x_1, y_1) and B (x_2, y_2) can be found using this formula: $M(\frac{x_1+x_2}{2}, \frac{y_1+y_2}{2})$
Example	Find the midpoint of the line segment with the given endpoints. $(1, -2), (3, 6)$ **Solution:** Midpoint $= (\frac{x_1+x_2}{2}, \frac{y_1+y_2}{2}) \rightarrow (x_1, y_1) = (1, -2)$ and $(x_2, y_2) = (3, 6)$ Midpoint $= (\frac{1+3}{2}, \frac{-2+6}{2}) \rightarrow (\frac{4}{2}, \frac{4}{2}) \rightarrow M(2, 2)$
Your Turn! **Find more at** bit.ly/3nPdnTq	1) $(2, 1), (-4, 1)$ *Midpoint* = (__, __) 2) $(6, -2), (2, 4)$ *Midpoint* = (__, __) 3) $(-3, 4), (-5, 0)$ *Midpoint* = (__, __) 4) $(8, 1), (-4, 5)$ *Midpoint* = (__, __) 5) $(6, 7), (-4, 5)$ *Midpoint* = (__, __) 6) $(2, -3), (2, 5)$ *Midpoint* = (__, __) 7) $(7, 3), (-1, -7)$ *Midpoint* = (__, __) 8) $(3, 9), (-1, 5)$ *Midpoint* = (__, __) 9) $(5, 2), (-9, 0)$ *Midpoint* = (__, __) 10) $(2, 7), (10, -9)$ *Midpoint* = (__, __)

Topic	Finding Midpoint – Answers
Notes	✓ The middle of a line segment is its midpoint. ✓ The Midpoint of two endpoints A (x_1, y_1) and B (x_2, y_2) can be found using this formula: $M(\frac{x_1+x_2}{2}, \frac{y_1+y_2}{2})$
Example	Find the midpoint of the line segment with the given endpoints. $(1, -2), (3, 6)$ **Solution:** Midpoint $= (\frac{x_1+x_2}{2}, \frac{y_1+y_2}{2}) \rightarrow (x_1, y_1) = (1, -2)$ and $(x_2, y_2) = (3, 6)$ Midpoint $= (\frac{1+3}{2}, \frac{-2+6}{2}) \rightarrow (\frac{4}{2}, \frac{4}{2}) \rightarrow M(2, 2)$

Your Turn!		
	1) $(2, 1), (-4, 1)$ **Midpoint** $= (-1, 1)$	2) $(6, -2), (2, 4)$ **Midpoint** $= (4, 1)$
	3) $(-3, 4), (-5, 0)$ **Midpoint** $= (-4, 2)$	4) $(8, 1), (-4, 5)$ **Midpoint** $= (2, 3)$
	5) $(6, 7), (-4, 5)$ **Midpoint** $= (1, 6)$	6) $(2, -3), (2, 5)$ **Midpoint** $= (2, 1)$
	7) $(7, 3), (-1, -7)$ **Midpoint** $= (3, -2)$	8) $(3, 9), (-1, 5)$ **Midpoint** $= (1, 7)$
Find more at bit.ly/3nPdnTq	9) $(5, 2), (-9, 0)$ **Midpoint** $= (-2, 1)$	10) $(2, 7), (10, -9)$ **Midpoint** $= (6, -1)$

Topic	**Finding Distance of Two Points**
Notes	✓ Use this formula to find the distance of two points A (x_1, y_1) and B (x_2, y_2): $$d = \sqrt{(x_2 - x_1)^2 + (y_2 - y_1)^2}$$
Example	*Find the distance of two points* $(-1, 5)$ and $(4, -7)$. **Solution:** *Use distance of two points formula:* $d = \sqrt{(x_2 - x_1)^2 + (y_2 - y_1)^2}$ $(x_1, y_1) = (-1, 5)$, and $(x_2, y_2) = (4, -7)$ Then: $d = \sqrt{(x_2 - x_1)^2 + (y_2 - y_1)^2} \rightarrow d =$ $\sqrt{(4 - (-1))^2 + (-7 - 5)^2} = \sqrt{(5)^2 + (-12)^2} = \sqrt{25 + 144} =$ $\sqrt{169} = 13$

Your Turn!	1) $(8, 2), (-6, 2)$ *Distance* = ____	2) $(3, -4), (3, 6)$ *Distance* = ____
	3) $(-5, 10), (7, 1)$ *Distance* = ____	4) $(8, 1), (-4, 6)$ *Distance* = ____
	5) $(-3, 6), (-4, 5)$ *Distance* = ____	6) $(4, -1), (14, 23)$ *Distance* = ____
Find more at bit.ly/2KV50Hy	7) $(3, 5), (6, 9)$ *Distance* = ____	8) $(2, -2), (10, 4)$ *Distance* = ____

Topic	Finding Distance of Two Points - Answers
Notes	✓ Use this formula to find the distance of two points A (x_1, y_1) and B (x_2, y_2): $$d = \sqrt{(x_2 - x_1)^2 + (y_2 - y_1)^2}$$
Example	*Find the distance of two points* $(-1, 5)$ and $(4, -7)$. **Solution:** *Use distance of two points formula:* $d = \sqrt{(x_2 - x_1)^2 + (y_2 - y_1)^2}$ $(x_1, y_1) = (-1, 5)$, and $(x_2, y_2) = (4, -7)$ Then: $d = \sqrt{(x_2 - x_1)^2 + (y_2 - y_1)^2} \rightarrow d = \sqrt{(4 - (-1))^2 + (-7 - 5)^2} = \sqrt{(5)^2 + (-12)^2} = \sqrt{25 + 144} = \sqrt{169} = 13$

Your Turn!		
	1) $(8, 2), (-6, 2)$ *Distance* $= 14$	2) $(3, -4), (3, 6)$ *Distance* $= 10$
	3) $(-5, 10), (7, 1)$ *Distance* $= 15$	4) $(8, 1), (-4, 6)$ *Distance* $= 13$
	5) $(-3, 6), (-4, 5)$ *Distance* $= \sqrt{2}$	6) $(4, -1), (14, 23)$ *Distance* $= 26$
	7) $(3, 5), (6, 9)$ *Distance* $= 5$	8) $(2, -2), (10, 4)$ *Distance* $= 10$

Find more at

bit.ly/2KV50Hy

Topic	**Multiplication Property of Exponents**
Notes	✓ Exponents are shorthand for repeated multiplication of the same number by itself. For example, instead of 2×2, we can write 2^2. For $3 \times 3 \times 3 \times 3$, we can write 3^4 ✓ In algebra, a variable is a letter used to stand for a number. The most common letters are: $x, y, z, a, b, c, m,$ and n. ✓ Exponent's rules: $x^a \times x^b = x^{a+b}$, $\dfrac{x^a}{x^b} = x^{a-b}$ $\qquad (x^a)^b = x^{a \times b} \qquad\qquad (xy)^a = x^a \times y^a \qquad \left(\dfrac{a}{b}\right)^c = \dfrac{a^c}{b^c}$
Example	**Multiply.** $4x^3 \times 2x^2$ Use Exponent's rules: $x^a \times x^b = x^{a+b} \rightarrow x^3 \times x^2 = x^{3+2} = x^5$ Then: $4x^3 \times 2x^2 = 8x^5$
Your Turn!	1) $x^2 \times 5x =$ 2) $3x^4 \times x^2 =$
	3) $3x^2 \times 4x^5 =$ 4) $3x^2 \times 6xy =$
	5) $3x^5y \times 5x^2y^3 =$ 6) $3x^2y^2 \times 5x^2y^8 =$
	7) $5x^2y \times 5x^2y^7 =$ 8) $6x^6 \times 4x^9y^4 =$
	9) $4x^2y^5 \times 6x^5y^3 =$ 10) $10x^6x^2 \times 7xy^5 =$

Find more at

bit.ly/34AWHr1

Topic	**Multiplication Property of Exponents - Answers**
Notes	✓ Exponents are shorthand for repeated multiplication of the same number by itself. For example, instead of 2×2, we can write 2^2. For $3 \times 3 \times 3 \times 3$, we can write 3^4 ✓ In algebra, a variable is a letter used to stand for a number. The most common letters are: $x, y, z, a, b, c, m, and\ n$. ✓ Exponent's rules: $x^a \times x^b = x^{a+b}$, $\frac{x^a}{x^b} = x^{a-b}$ $(x^a)^b = x^{a \times b}$ $(xy)^a = x^a \times y^a$ $\left(\frac{a}{b}\right)^c = \frac{a^c}{b^c}$
Example	***Multiply.*** $4x^3 \times 2x^2$ Use Exponent's rules: $x^a \times x^b = x^{a+b} \rightarrow x^3 \times x^2 = x^{3+2} = x^5$ Then: $4x^3 \times 2x^2 = 8x^5$

Your Turn!		
	1) $x^2 \times 5x = 5x^3$	2) $3x^4 \times x^2 = 3x^6$
	3) $3x^2 \times 4x^5 = 12x^7$	4) $3x^2 \times 6xy = 18x^3y$
	5) $3x^5y \times 5x^2y^3 = 15x^7y^4$	6) $3x^2y^2 \times 5x^2y^8 = 15x^4y^{10}$
	7) $5x^2y \times 5x^2y^7 = 25x^4y^8$	8) $6x^6 \times 4x^9y^4 = 24x^{15}y^4$
Find more at bit.ly/34AWHr1	9) $4x^2y^5 \times 6x^5y^3 = 24x^7y^8$	10) $10x^6x^2 \times 7xy^5 = 70x^9y^5$

Topic	Division Property of Exponents
Notes	✓ For division of exponents use these formulas: $\frac{x^a}{x^b} = x^{a-b}$, $x \neq 0$ $\frac{x^a}{x^b} = \frac{1}{x^{b-a}}$, $x \neq 0$, $\frac{1}{x^b} = x^{-b}$
Example	*Simplify.* $\frac{6x^3y}{36x^2y^3}$ First cancel the common factor: $6 \to \frac{6x^3y}{36x^2y^3} = \frac{x^3y}{6x^2y^3}$ Use Exponent's rules: $\frac{x^a}{x^b} = x^{a-b} \to \frac{x^3}{x^2} = x^{3-2} = x^1 = x$ Then: $\frac{6x^3y}{36x^2y^3} = \frac{xy}{6y^3} \to$ now cancel the common factor: $y \to \frac{xy}{6y^3} = \frac{x}{6y^2}$
Your Turn! **Find more at** bit.ly/37JAcIZ	1) $\frac{2^5}{2^2} =$ 2) $\frac{6x}{12x^3} =$ 3) $\frac{3x^3}{2x^5} =$ 4) $\frac{12x^3}{14x^6} =$ 5) $\frac{12x^3}{9y^8} =$ 6) $\frac{25xy^4}{5x^6y^2} =$ 7) $\frac{2x^4y^5}{7xy^2} =$ 8) $\frac{16x^2y^8}{4x^3} =$ 9) $\frac{9x^4}{12x^7y^9} =$ 10) $\frac{14y^8x^4}{21y^2x^8} =$

Topic	Division Property of Exponents - Answers
Notes	✓ For division of exponents use following formulas: $\dfrac{x^a}{x^b} = x^{a-b}$, $x \neq 0$ $\dfrac{x^a}{x^b} = \dfrac{1}{x^{b-a}}$, $x \neq 0$, $\qquad \dfrac{1}{x^b} = x^{-b}$
Example	*Simplify.* $\dfrac{6x^3y}{36x^2y^3}$ First cancel the common factor: $6 \rightarrow \dfrac{6x^3y}{36x^2y^3} = \dfrac{x^3y}{6x^2y^3}$ Use Exponent's rules: $\dfrac{x^a}{x^b} = x^{a-b} \rightarrow \dfrac{x^3}{x^2} = x^{3-2} = x^1 = x$ Then: $\dfrac{6x^3y}{36x^2y^3} = \dfrac{xy}{6y^3} \rightarrow$ now cancel the common factor: $y \rightarrow \dfrac{xy}{6y^3} = \dfrac{x}{6y^2}$

Your Turn!	1) $\dfrac{2^5}{2^2} = 2^3$	2) $\dfrac{6x}{12x^3} = \dfrac{1}{2x^2}$
	3) $\dfrac{3x^3}{2x^5} = \dfrac{3}{2x^2}$	4) $\dfrac{12x^3}{14x^6} = \dfrac{6}{7x^3}$
	5) $\dfrac{12x^3}{9y^8} = \dfrac{4x^3}{3y^8}$	6) $\dfrac{25xy^4}{5x^6y^2} = \dfrac{5y^2}{x^5}$
	7) $\dfrac{2x^4y^5}{7xy^2} = \dfrac{2x^3y^3}{7}$	8) $\dfrac{16x^2y^8}{4x^3} = \dfrac{4y^8}{x}$
Find more at bit.ly/37JAclZ 	9) $\dfrac{9x^4}{12x^7y^9} = \dfrac{3}{4x^3y^9}$	10) $\dfrac{14y^8x^4}{21y^2x^8} = \dfrac{2y^6}{3x^4}$

Topic	**Powers of Products and Quotients**
Notes	✓ For any nonzero numbers a and b and any integer x, $$(ab)^x = a^x \times b^x, \left(\frac{a}{b}\right)^c = \frac{a^c}{b^c}$$
Example	***Simplify.*** $\left(\frac{2x^3}{x}\right)^2$ First cancel the common factor: $x \rightarrow \left(\frac{2x^3}{x}\right)^2 = (2x^2)^2$ Use Exponent's rules: $(ab)^x = a^x \times b^x$ Then: $(2x^2)^2 = (2)^2(x^2)^2 = 4x^4$

Your Turn!	1) $(3x^3x^3)^3 =$	2) $(2x^3 \times 6x)^2 =$
	3) $(10x^{11}y^3)^2 =$	4) $(9x^7y^5)^2 =$
	5) $(4x^4y^6)^3 =$	6) $(3x \times 4y^3)^2 =$
	7) $\left(\frac{5x}{x^2}\right)^2 =$	8) $\left(\frac{x^4y^4}{x^2y^2}\right)^3 =$
Find more at bit.ly/34CgPJm	9) $\left(\frac{24x}{4x^6}\right)^2 =$	10) $\left(\frac{x^6}{x^4y^2}\right)^2 =$

Topic	Powers of Products and Quotients - Answers
Notes	✓ For any nonzero numbers a and b and any integer x, $$(ab)^x = a^x \times b^x, \left(\frac{a}{b}\right)^c = \frac{a^c}{b^c}$$
Example	*Simplify.* $\left(\frac{2x^3}{x}\right)^2$ First cancel the common factor: $x \rightarrow \left(\frac{2x^3}{x}\right)^2 = (2x^2)^2$ Use Exponent's rules: $(ab)^x = a^x \times b^x$ Then: $(2x^2)^2 = (2)^2(x^2)^2 = 4x^4$

Your Turn!		
	1) $(3x^3x^3)^3 = 27x^{18}$	2) $(2x^3 \times 6x)^2 = 144x^8$
	3) $(10x^{11}y^3)^2 =$ $100x^{22}y^6$	4) $(9x^7y^5)^2 = 81x^{14}y^{10}$
	5) $(4x^4y^6)^3 = 64\,x^{12}y^{18}$	6) $(3x \times 4y^3)^2 = 144x^2y^6$
Find more at bit.ly/34CgPJm	7) $\left(\frac{5x}{x^2}\right)^2 = \frac{25}{x^2}$	8) $\left(\frac{x^4y^4}{x^2y^2}\right)^3 = x^6y^6$
	9) $\left(\frac{24x}{4x^6}\right)^2 = \frac{36}{x^{10}}$	10) $\left(\frac{x^6}{x^4y^2}\right)^2 = \frac{x^4}{y^4}$

Topic	Zero and Negative Exponents
Notes	✓ A negative exponent is the reciprocal of that number with a positive exponent. $(3)^{-2} = \frac{1}{3^2}$ ✓ Zero-Exponent Rule: $a^0 = 1$, this means that anything raised to the zero power is 1. For example: $(28x^2y)^0 = 1$
Example	***Evaluate.*** $\left(\frac{1}{3}\right)^{-2} =$ Use negative exponent's rule: $\left(\frac{1}{x^a}\right)^{-2} = (x^a)^2 \rightarrow \left(\frac{1}{3}\right)^{-2} = (3)^2 =$ Then: $(3)^2 = 9$

Your Turn!	1) $2^{-4} =$	2) $4^{-3} =$
	3) $7^{-3} =$	4) $1^{-3} =$
	5) $8^{-3} =$	6) $4^{-4} =$
	7) $10^{-3} =$	8) $7^{-4} =$
Find more at bit.ly/3rnkh4	9) $\left(\frac{1}{6}\right)^{-1} =$	10) $\left(\frac{1}{9}\right)^{-2} =$

Topic	Zero and Negative Exponents - Answers
Notes	✓ A negative exponent is the reciprocal of that number with a positive exponent. $(3)^{-2} = \frac{1}{3^2}$ ✓ Zero-Exponent Rule: $a^0 = 1$, this means that anything raised to the zero power is 1. For example: $(28x^2y)^0 = 1$
Example	**Evaluate.** $\left(\frac{1}{3}\right)^{-2} =$ Use negative exponent's rule: $\left(\frac{1}{x^a}\right)^{-2} = (x^a)^2 \rightarrow \left(\frac{1}{3}\right)^{-2} = (3)^2 =$ Then: $(3)^2 = 9$

Your Turn!		
	1) $2^{-4} = \frac{1}{16}$	2) $4^{-3} = \frac{1}{64}$
	3) $7^{-3} = \frac{1}{343}$	4) $1^{-3} = 1$
	5) $8^{-3} = \frac{1}{512}$	6) $4^{-4} = \frac{1}{256}$
	7) $10^{-3} = \frac{1}{1,000}$	8) $7^{-4} = \frac{1}{2,401}$
	9) $\left(\frac{1}{6}\right)^{-1} = 6$	10) $\left(\frac{1}{9}\right)^{-2} = 81$

Find more at

bit.ly/3rnkh4

Topic	**Negative Exponents and Negative Bases**
Notes	✓ Make the power positive. A negative exponent is the reciprocal of that number with a positive exponent. ✓ The parenthesis is important! 5^{-2} is not the same as $(-5)^{-2}$ $$(-5)^{-2} = -\frac{1}{5^2} \text{ and } (-5)^{-2} = +\frac{1}{5^2}$$
Example	***Simplify.*** $\left(-\frac{3x}{4yz}\right)^{-3} =$ Use negative exponent's rule: $\left(\frac{x^a}{x^b}\right)^{-2} = \left(\frac{x^b}{x^a}\right)^2 \rightarrow \left(-\frac{3x}{4yz}\right)^{-3} = \left(-\frac{4yz}{3x}\right)^3$ Now use exponent's rule: $\left(\frac{a}{b}\right)^c = \frac{a^c}{b^c} \rightarrow \left(-\frac{4yz}{3x}\right)^3 = -\frac{4^3 y^3 z^3}{3^3 x^3} = -\frac{64 y^3 z^3}{27 x^3}$
Your Turn!	1) $-4x^{-3}y^{-3} =$ 2) $25x^{-4}y^{-2} =$
	3) $14a^{-6}b^{-7} =$ 4) $-12x^2y^{-3} =$
	5) $-\frac{25}{x^{-6}} =$ 6) $\frac{7b}{-9c^{-4}} =$
	7) $\frac{7ab}{a^{-3}b^{-1}} =$ 8) $-\frac{5n^{-2}}{10p^{-3}} = -$
	9) $\frac{36ab^{-1}}{-3c^{-2}} =$ 10) $\left(\frac{5a}{3c}\right)^{-2} =$

Find more at
bit.ly/3nPROSM

Topic	Negative Exponents and Negative Bases - Answers
Notes	✓ Make the power positive. A negative exponent is the reciprocal of that number with a positive exponent. ✓ The parenthesis is important! 5^{-2} is not the same as $(-5)^{-2}$ $$(-5)^{-2} = -\frac{1}{5^2} \text{ and } (-5)^{-2} = +\frac{1}{5^2}$$
Example	*Simplify*. $\left(-\frac{3x}{4yz}\right)^{-3} =$ Use negative exponent's rule: $\left(\frac{x^a}{x^b}\right)^{-2} = \left(\frac{x^b}{x^a}\right)^2 \rightarrow \left(-\frac{3x}{4yz}\right)^{-3} = \left(-\frac{4yz}{3x}\right)^3$ Now use exponent's rule: $\left(\frac{a}{b}\right)^c = \frac{a^c}{b^c} \rightarrow \left(-\frac{4yz}{3x}\right)^3 = -\frac{4^3 y^3 z^3}{3^3 x^3} = -\frac{64 y^3 z^3}{27 x^3}$

Your Turn!		
	1) $-4x^{-3}y^{-3} = -\dfrac{4}{x^3 y^3}$	2) $25x^{-4}y^{-2} = \dfrac{25}{x^4 y^2}$
	3) $14a^{-6}b^{-7} = \dfrac{14}{a^6 b^7}$	4) $-12x^2 y^{-3} = -\dfrac{12x^2}{y^3}$
	5) $-\dfrac{25}{x^{-6}} = -25x^6$	6) $\dfrac{7b}{-9c^{-4}} = -\dfrac{7bc^4}{9}$
	7) $\dfrac{7ab}{a^{-3}b^{-1}} = 7a^4 b^2$	8) $-\dfrac{5n^{-2}}{10p^{-3}} = -\dfrac{p^3}{2n^2}$
	9) $\dfrac{36ab^{-1}}{-3c^{-2}} = -\dfrac{12ac^2}{b}$	10) $\left(\dfrac{5a}{3c}\right)^{-2} = \dfrac{9c^2}{25a^2}$

Find more at

bit.ly/3nPROSM

Topic	Scientific Notation
Notes	✓ It is used to write very big or very small numbers in decimal form. ✓ In scientific notation all numbers are written in the form of: $$m \times 10^n$$ <table><tr><th>Decimal notation</th><th>Scientific notation</th></tr><tr><td>3</td><td>3×10^0</td></tr><tr><td>$-45,000$</td><td>-4.5×10^4</td></tr><tr><td>0.3</td><td>3×10^{-1}</td></tr><tr><td>2,122.456</td><td>2.122456×10^3</td></tr></table>
Example	*Write* 0.00054 *in scientific notation.* First, move the decimal point to the right so that you have a number that is between 1 and 10. Then: $m = 5.4$ Now, determine how many places the decimal moved in step 1 by the power of 10. Then: $10^{-4} \rightarrow$ When the decimal moved to the right, the exponent is negative. Then: $0.00054 = 5.4 \times 10^{-4}$

Your Turn!		
	1) $0.000452 =$	2) $0.00016 =$
	3) $52,000,000 =$	4) $21,000 =$
Find more at bit.ly/3nOwJYP	5) $3 \times 10^{-1} =$	6) $5 \times 10^{-2} =$
	7) $1.4 \times 10^4 =$	8) $3 \times 10^{-5} =$

Topic	Scientific Notation – Answers
Notes	✓ It is used to write very big or very small numbers in decimal form. ✓ In scientific notation all numbers are written in the form of: $$m \times 10^n$$ <table><tr><td>Decimal notation</td><td>Scientific notation</td></tr><tr><td>3</td><td>3×10^0</td></tr><tr><td>$-45,000$</td><td>-4.5×10^4</td></tr><tr><td>0.3</td><td>3×10^{-1}</td></tr><tr><td>2,122.456</td><td>2.122456×10^3</td></tr></table>
Example	*Write 0.00054 in scientific notation.* First, move the decimal point to the right so that you have a number that is between 1 and 10. Then: $m = 5.4$ Now, determine how many places the decimal moved in step 1 by the power of 10. Then: $10^{-4} \rightarrow$ When the decimal moved to the right, the exponent is negative. Then: $0.00054 = 5.4 \times 10^{-4}$

Your Turn!		
	1) $0.000452 = 4.52 \times 10^{-4}$	2) $0.00016 = 1.6 \times 10^{-4}$
	3) $52,000,000 = 5.2 \times 10^7$	4) $21,000 = 2.1 \times 10^4$
Find more at bit.ly/3nOwJYP	5) $3 \times 10^{-1} = 0.3$	6) $5 \times 10^{-2} = 0.05$
	7) $1.4 \times 10^4 = 14,000$	8) $3 \times 10^{-5} = 0.00003$

Topic	Radicals
Notes	✓ If n is a positive integer and x is a real number, then: $\sqrt[n]{x} = x^{\frac{1}{n}}$, $\sqrt[n]{xy} = x^{\frac{1}{n}} \times y^{\frac{1}{n}}$, $\sqrt[n]{\frac{x}{y}} = \frac{x^{\frac{1}{n}}}{y^{\frac{1}{n}}}$, and $\sqrt[n]{x} \times \sqrt[n]{y} = \sqrt[n]{xy}$ ✓ A square root of x is a number r whose square is: $r^2 = x$ (r is a square root of x. ✓ To add and subtract radicals, we need to have the same values under the radical. For example: $\sqrt{3} + \sqrt{3} = 2\sqrt{3}$, $3\sqrt{5} - \sqrt{5} = 2\sqrt{5}$
Example	*Evaluate.* $\sqrt{32} + \sqrt{8} =$ **Solution:** Since we do not have the same values under the radical, we cannot add these two radicals. But we can simplify each radical. $\sqrt{32} = \sqrt{16} \times \sqrt{2} = 4\sqrt{2}$ and $\sqrt{8} = \sqrt{4} \times \sqrt{2} = 2\sqrt{2}$ Now, we have the same values under the radical. Then: $$\sqrt{32} + \sqrt{8} = 4\sqrt{2} + 2\sqrt{2} = 6\sqrt{2}$$

Your Turn!		
	1) $\sqrt{6} \times \sqrt{6} =$	2) $\sqrt{12} \times \sqrt{3} =$
	3) $\sqrt{3} \times \sqrt{27} =$	4) $\sqrt{32} \div \sqrt{2} =$
	5) $\sqrt{2} + \sqrt{8} =$	6) $\sqrt{27} - \sqrt{3} =$
	7) $3\sqrt{7} - 2\sqrt{7} =$	8) $6\sqrt{5} \times 3\sqrt{5} =$

Find more at

bit.ly/2WEATgr

Topic	Radicals - Answers
Notes	✓ If n is a positive integer and x is a real number, then: $\sqrt[n]{x} = x^{\frac{1}{n}}$, $\sqrt[n]{xy} = x^{\frac{1}{n}} \times y^{\frac{1}{n}}$, $\sqrt[n]{\frac{x}{y}} = \frac{x^{\frac{1}{n}}}{y^{\frac{1}{n}}}$, and $\sqrt[n]{x} \times \sqrt[n]{y} = \sqrt[n]{xy}$ ✓ A square root of x is a number r whose square is: $r^2 = x$ (r is a square root of x. ✓ To add and subtract radicals, we need to have the same values under the radical. For example: $\sqrt{3} + \sqrt{3} = 2\sqrt{3}$, $3\sqrt{5} - \sqrt{5} = 2\sqrt{5}$
Example	***Evaluate.*** $\sqrt{32} + \sqrt{8} =$ **Solution:** Since we do not have the same values under the radical, we cannot add these two radicals. But we can simplify each radical. $\sqrt{32} = \sqrt{16} \times \sqrt{2} = 4\sqrt{2}$ and $\sqrt{8} = \sqrt{4} \times \sqrt{2} = 2\sqrt{2}$ Now, we have the same values under the radical. Then: $$\sqrt{32} + \sqrt{8} = 4\sqrt{2} + 2\sqrt{2} = 6\sqrt{2}$$

Your Turn!		
	1) $\sqrt{6} \times \sqrt{6} = 6$	2) $\sqrt{12} \times \sqrt{3} = 6$
	3) $\sqrt{3} \times \sqrt{27} = 9$	4) $\sqrt{32} \div \sqrt{2} = 4$
Find more at bit.ly/2WEATqr	5) $\sqrt{2} + \sqrt{8} = 3\sqrt{2}$	6) $\sqrt{27} - \sqrt{3} = 2\sqrt{3}$
	7) $3\sqrt{7} - 2\sqrt{7} = \sqrt{7}$	8) $6\sqrt{5} \times 3\sqrt{5} = 90$

Topic	Simplifying Polynomials
Notes	✓ Find "like" terms. (they have same variables with same power). ✓ Use "FOIL". (First–Out–In–Last) for binomials: $$(x + a)(x + b) = x^2 + (b + a)x + ab$$ ✓ Add or Subtract "like" terms using order of operation.
Example	***Simplify this expression***. $(x + 3)(x - 8) =$ **Solution:** First apply FOIL method: $(a + b)(c + d) = ac + ad + bc + bd$ $(x + 3)(x - 8) = x^2 - 8x + 3x - 24$ Now combine like terms: $x^2 - 8x + 3x - 24 = x^2 - 5x - 24$

Your Turn!	1) $-(4x - 3) =$ _____	2) $3(4x + 7) =$ _____
	3) $3x(3x - 4) =$ _____	4) $5x(2x + 8) =$ _____
	5) $-2x(5x + 6) + 5x =$ _____	6) $-4x(8x - 3) - x^2 =$ _____
Find more at bit.ly/3rnAcj8	7) $(x + 4)(x + 5) =$ _____	8) $(x + 2)(x + 8) =$ _____
	9) $-5x^2 + 9x^3 + 10x^2 =$ _____	10) $-6x^5 + 8x^4 + 9x^5 =$ _____

Topic	Simplifying Polynomials – Answers
Notes	✓ Find "like" terms. (they have same variables with same power). ✓ Use "FOIL". (First–Out–In–Last) for binomials: $$(x + a)(x + b) = x^2 + (b + a)x + ab$$ ✓ Add or Subtract "like" terms using order of operation.
Example	*Simplify this expression*. $(x + 3)(x - 8) =$ **Solution:** First apply FOIL method: $(a + b)(c + d) = ac + ad + bc + bd$ $(x + 3)(x - 8) = x^2 - 8x + 3x - 24$ Now combine like terms: $x^2 - 8x + 3x - 24 = x^2 - 5x - 24$

Your Turn!		
	1) $-(4x - 3) =$ $-4x + 3$	2) $3(4x + 7) =$ $12x + 21$
	3) $3x(3x - 4) =$ $9x^2 - 12x$	4) $5x(2x + 8) =$ $10x^2 + 40x$
	5) $-2x(5x + 6) + 5x =$ $-10x^2 - 7x$	6) $-4x(8x - 3) - x^2 =$ $-33x^2 + 12x$
Find more at bit.ly/3rnAcj8	7) $(x + 4)(x + 5) =$ $x^2 + 9x + 20$	8) $(x + 2)(x + 8) =$ $x^2 + 10x + 16$
	9) $-5x^2 + 9x^3 + 10x^2 =$ $9x^3 + 5x^2$	10) $-6x^5 + 8x^4 + 9x^5 =$ $3x^5 + 8x^4$

Topic	Adding and Subtracting Polynomials
Notes	✓ Adding polynomials is just a matter of combining like terms, with some order of operations considerations thrown in. ✓ Be careful with the minus signs, and don't confuse addition and multiplication!
Example	*Simplify the expressions.* $(3x^2 - 4x^3) - (5x^3 - 8x^2) =$ **Solution:** First use Distributive Property: $-(5x^3 - 8x^2) = -5x^3 + 8x^2$ $\rightarrow (3x^2 - 4x^3) - (5x^3 - 8x^2) = 3x^2 - 4x^3 - 5x^3 + 8x^2$ Now combine like terms: $3x^2 - 4x^3 - 5x^3 + 8x^2 = -9x^3 + 11x^2$

Your Turn!

1) $(x^2 - 3x) + (2x^2 - 6) =$ _____	2) $(4x^3 + 2x) - (x^3 + 5) =$ _____
3) $(x^2 - 5x) + (6x^2 - 5) =$ _____	4) $(8x^2 - 2) - (3x^2 + 7) =$ _____
5) $(3x^2 + 2) - (2 - 4x^2) =$ _____	6) $(x^3 + x^2) - (x^3 - 10) =$ _____
7) $(3x^3 - 2x) - (x - x^3) =$ _____	8) $(x - 5x^4) - (2x^4 + 3x) =$ _____
9) $(8x^3 + 3) - (5 - 4x^3) =$ _____	10) $(9x^2 + 4x^3) - (3x^3 + 2) =$

Find more at

bit.ly/2KUqHqQ

Topic	Adding and Subtracting Polynomials – Answers
Notes	✓ Adding polynomials is just a matter of combining like terms, with some order of operations considerations thrown in. ✓ Be careful with the minus signs, and don't confuse addition and multiplication!
Example	*Simplify the expressions.* $(3x^2 - 4x^3) - (5x^3 - 8x^2) =$ **Solution:** First use Distributive Property: $-(5x^3 - 8x^2) = -5x^3 + 8x^2$ $\rightarrow (3x^2 - 4x^3) - (5x^3 - 8x^2) = 3x^2 - 4x^3 - 5x^3 + 8x^2$ Now combine like terms: $3x^2 - 4x^3 - 5x^3 + 8x^2 = -9x^3 + 11x^2$

Your Turn!	1) $(x^2 - 3x) + (2x^2 - 6) =$ $3x^2 - 3x - 6$	2) $(4x^3 + 2x) - (x^3 + 5) =$ $3x^3 + 2x - 5$
	3) $(x^2 - 5x) + (6x^2 - 5) =$ $7x^2 - 5x - 5$	4) $(8x^2 - 2) - (3x^2 + 7) =$ $5x^2 - 9$
	5) $(3x^2 + 2) - (2 - 4x^2) =$ $7x^2$	6) $(x^3 + x^2) - (x^3 - 10) =$ $x^2 + 10$
Find more at bit.ly/2KUqHqQ	7) $(3x^3 - 2x) - (x - x^3) =$ $4x^3 - 3x$	8) $(x - 5x^4) - (2x^4 + 3x) =$ $-7x^4 - 2x$
	9) $(8x^3 + 3) - (5 - 4x^3) =$ $12x^3 - 2$	10) $(9x^2 + 4x^3) - (3x^3 + 2) =$ $x^3 + 9x^2 - 2$

Topic	**Multiplying Binomials**
Notes	✓A binomial is a polynomial that is the sum or the difference of two terms, each of which is a monomial. ✓To multiply two binomials, use "FOIL" method. (First–Out–In–Last) $(x + a)(x + b) = x \times x + x \times b + a \times x + a \times b = x^2 + bx + ax + ab$
Example	*Multiply.* $(x - 4)(x + 9) =$ **Solution:** Use "FOIL". (First–Out–In–Last): $(x - 4)(x + 9) = x^2 + 9x - 4x - 36$ Then simplify: $x^2 + 9x - 4x - 36 = x^2 + 5x - 36$
Your Turn!	1) $(x + 4)(x + 4) =$ _____ 2) $(x + 4)(x + 3) =$ _____ 3) $(x - 3)(x + 4) =$ _____ 4) $(x - 2)(x - 4) =$ _____ 5) $(x + 3)(x + 4) =$ _____ 6) $(x + 5)(x + 4) =$ _____ 7) $(x - 6)(x - 5) =$ _____ 8) $(x - 5)(x - 5) =$ _____ 9) $(x + 3)(x - 5) =$ _____ 10) $(x - 6)(x + 4) =$ _____

Find more at

bit.ly/3aCsOFL

Topic	Multiplying Binomials – Answers
Notes	✓ A binomial is a polynomial that is the sum or the difference of two terms, each of which is a monomial. ✓ To multiply two binomials, use "FOIL" method. (First–Out–In–Last) $$(x + a)(x + b) = x \times x + x \times b + a \times x + a \times b = x^2 + bx + ax + ab$$
Example	*Multiply.* $(x - 4)(x + 9) =$ **Solution:** Use "FOIL". (First–Out–In–Last): $(x - 4)(x + 9) = x^2 + 9x - 4x - 36$ Then simplify: $x^2 + 9x - 4x - 36 = x^2 + 5x - 36$

Your Turn!		
Find more at bit.ly/3aCsOFL	1) $(x + 4)(x + 4) =$ $x^2 + 8x + 16$	2) $(x + 4)(x + 3) =$ $x^2 + 7x + 12$
	3) $(x - 3)(x + 4) =$ $x^2 + x - 12$	4) $(x - 2)(x - 4) =$ $x^2 - 6x + 8$
	5) $(x + 3)(x + 4) =$ $x^2 + 7x + 12$	6) $(x + 5)(x + 4) =$ $x^2 + 9x + 20$
	7) $(x - 6)(x - 5) =$ $x^2 - 11x + 30$	8) $(x - 5)(x - 5) =$ $x^2 - 10x + 25$
	9) $(x + 3)(x - 5) =$ $x^2 - 2x - 15$	10) $(x - 6)(x + 4) =$ $x^2 - 2x - 24$

Topic	**Multiplying and Dividing Monomials**
Notes	✓ When you divide or multiply two monomials you need to divide or multiply their coefficients and then divide or multiply their variables. ✓ In case of exponents with the same base, you need to subtract their powers. ✓ Exponent's rules: $$x^a \times x^b = x^{a+b}, \qquad \frac{x^a}{x^b} = x^{a-b}$$ $$\frac{1}{x^b} = x^{-b}, \quad (x^a)^b = x^{a \times b}$$ $$(xy)^a = x^a \times y^a$$
Example	***Divide expressions.*** $\frac{-18x^5y^6}{2xy^2} =$ **Solution:** Use exponents' division rule: $\frac{x^a}{x^b} = x^{a-b}, \frac{x^5}{x} = x^{5-1} = x^4$ and $\frac{y^6}{y^2} = y^4$ Then: $\frac{-18x^5y^6}{2xy^2} = -9x^4y^4$
Your Turn! **Find more at** bit.ly/2WHp4Q4	1) $(x^6y)(xy^3) =$ ___ 2) $(x^5y^2)(x^3y^3) =$ ___ 3) $(x^7y^4)(2x^5y^2) =$ ___ 4) $(3x^5y^4)(4x^6y^3) =$ ___ 5) $(-6x^8y^7)(4x^6y^9) =$ ___ 6) $(-2x^9y^3)(9x^7y^8) =$ ___ 7) $\frac{40x^9y^6}{8x^5y^4} =$ ___ 8) $\frac{-56x^{10}y^{15}}{8x^8y^9} =$ ___

Topic	**Multiplying and Dividing Monomials - Answers**
Notes	✓ When you divide or multiply two monomials you need to divide or multiply their coefficients and then divide or multiply their variables. ✓ In case of exponents with the same base, you need to subtract their powers. ✓ Exponent's rules: $$x^a \times x^b = x^{a+b}, \qquad \frac{x^a}{x^b} = x^{a-b}$$ $$\frac{1}{x^b} = x^{-b}, \quad (x^a)^b = x^{a \times b}$$ $$(xy)^a = x^a \times y^a$$
Example	***Divide expressions.*** $\frac{-18x^5y^6}{2xy^2} =$ **Solution:** Use exponents' division rule: $\frac{x^a}{x^b} = x^{a-b}, \frac{x^5}{x} = x^{5-1} = x^4$ and $\frac{y^6}{y^2} = y^4$ Then: $\frac{-18x^5y^6}{2xy^2} = -9x^4y^4$
Your Turn! **Find more at** bit.ly/2WHp4Q4 	1) $(x^6y)(xy^3) =$ $\quad x^7y^4$ 2) $(x^5y^2)(x^3y^3) =$ $\quad x^8y^5$ 3) $(x^7y^4)(2x^5y^2) =$ $\quad 2x^{12}y^6$ 4) $(3x^5y^4)(4x^6y^3) =$ $\quad 12x^{11}y^7$ 5) $(-6x^8y^7)(4x^6y^9) =$ $\quad -24x^{14}y^{16}$ 6) $(-2x^9y^3)(9x^7y^8) =$ $\quad -18x^{16}y^{11}$ 7) $\frac{40x^9y^6}{8x^5y^4} =$ $\quad 5x^4y^2$ 8) $\frac{-56x^{10}y^{15}}{8x^8y^9} =$ $\quad -7x^2y^6$

Topic	Multiplying a Polynomial and a Monomial
Notes	✓ When multiplying monomials, use the product rule for exponents. $x^a \times x^b = x^{a+b}$ ✓ When multiplying a monomial by a polynomial, use the distributive property. $$a \times (b + c) = a \times b + a \times c = ab + ac$$ $$a \times (b - c) = a \times b - a \times c = ab - ac$$
Example	*Multiply expressions.* $4x(5x - 8) =$ **Solution:** Use Distributive Property: $4x(5x - 8) = 4x \times 5x - 4x \times (8) =$ Now, simplify: $4x \times 5x - 4x \times (8) = 20x^2 - 32x$

Your Turn!	1) $4x(3x + y) =$ ____	2) $x(x - 6y) =$ ____
	3) $-x(5x - 3y) =$ ____	4) $4x(x + 5y) =$ ____
	5) $-x(5x + 8y) =$ ____	6) $2x(6x - 7y) =$ ____
Find more at bit.ly/3aBYdx2	7) $-4x(x^3 + 3y^2 - 7x) =$ ____	8) $6x(x^2 - 4y^2 + 3) =$ ____

Topic	**Multiplying a Polynomial and a Monomial - Answers**
Notes	✓ When multiplying monomials, use the product rule for exponents. $x^a \times x^b = x^{a+b}$ ✓ When multiplying a monomial by a polynomial, use the distributive property. $$a \times (b + c) = a \times b + a \times c = ab + ac$$ $$a \times (b - c) = a \times b - a \times c = ab - ac$$
Example	***Multiply expressions.*** $4x(5x - 8) =$ **Solution:** Use Distributive Property: $4x(5x - 8) = 4x \times 5x - 4x \times (8) =$ Now, simplify: $4x \times 5x - 4x \times (8) = 20x^2 - 32x$

Your Turn!	1) $4x(3x + y) =$ $12x^2 + 4xy$	2) $x(x - 6y) =$ $\qquad x^2 - 6xy$
	3) $-x(5x - 3y) =$ $-5x^2 + 3xy$	4) $4x(x + 5y) =$ $4x^2 + 20xy$
	5) $-x(5x + 8y) =$ $-5x^2 - 8xy$	6) $2x(6x - 7y) =$ $12x^2 - 14xy$
Find more at bit.ly/3aBYdx2	7) $-4x(x^3 + 3y^2 - 7x) =$ $-4x^4 - 12xy^2 + 28x^2$	8) $6x(x^2 - 4y^2 + 3) =$ $6x^3 - 24xy^2 + 18x$

Topic	**Multiplying Monomials**
Notes	✓ A monomial is a polynomial with just one term: Examples: $5x$ or $7x^2yz^8$ ✓ When you multiply monomials, first multiply the coefficients (a number placed before and multiplying the variable) and then multiply the variables using multiplication property of exponents. $x^a \times x^b = x^{a+b}$
Example	***Multiply.*** $(-3xy^4z^5) \times (2x^2y^5z^2) =$ **Solution:** Multiply coefficients and find same variables and use multiplication property of exponents: $x^a \times x^b = x^{a+b}$ $-3 \times 2 = -6$, $x \times x^2 = x^{1+2} = x^3$, $y^4 \times y^5 = y^{4+5} = y^9$, and $z^2 \times z^5 = z^{2+5} = z^7$ Then: $(-3xy^4z^5) \times (2x^2y^5z^2) = -6x^3y^9z^7$
Your Turn!	1) $3x^2 \times 5x^6 =$ _____ 2) $6x^7 \times 2x^4 =$ _____ 3) $-2x^2y^4 \times 6x^3y^2 =$ _____ 4) $-5x^5y \times 3x^3y^4 =$ _____ 5) $8x^7y^5 \times 5x^6y^3 =$ _____ 6) $-6x^7y^5 \times (-3x^9y^8) =$ _____ 7) $14x^8y^8z^4 \times 2x^4y^3z =$ _____ 8) $-7x^9y^7z^{11} \times 6x^6y^7z^5 =$ _____

Find more at

bit.ly/2KLVoP8

Topic	Multiplying Monomials- Answers
Notes	✓ A monomial is a polynomial with just one term: Examples: $5x$ or $7x^2yz^8$ ✓ When you multiply monomials, first multiply the coefficients (a number placed before and multiplying the variable) and then multiply the variables using multiplication property of exponents. $x^a \times x^b = x^{a+b}$
Example	*Multiply.* $(-3xy^4z^5) \times (2x^2y^5z^2) =$ **Solution:** Multiply coefficients and find same variables and use multiplication property of exponents: $x^a \times x^b = x^{a+b}$ $-3 \times 2 = -6$, $x \times x^2 = x^{1+2} = x^3$, $y^4 \times y^5 = y^{4+5} = y^9$, and $z^2 \times z^5 = z^{2+5} = z^7$ Then: $(-3xy^4z^5) \times (2x^2y^5z^2) = -6x^3y^9z^7$

Your Turn!		
	1) $3x^2 \times 5x^6 =$ $15x^8$	2) $6x^7 \times 2x^4 =$ $12x^{11}$
	3) $-2x^2y^4 \times 6x^3y^2 =$ $-12x^5y^6$	4) $-5x^5y \times 3x^3y^4 =$ $-15x^8y^5$
Find more at bit.ly/2KLVoP8	5) $8x^7y^5 \times 5x^6y^3 =$ $40x^{13}y^8$	6) $-6x^7y^5 \times (-3x^9y^8) =$ $18x^{16}y^{13}$
	7) $14x^8y^8z^4 \times 2x^4y^3z =$ $28x^{12}y^{11}z^5$	8) $-7x^9y^7z^{11} \times 6x^6y^7z^5 =$ $-42x^{15}y^{14}z^{16}$

Topic	Factoring Trinomials
Notes	To factor trinomial, use of the following methods: ✓ "FOIL": $(x + a)(x + b) = x^2 + (b + a)x + ab$ ✓ "Difference of Squares": $$a^2 - b^2 = (a + b)(a - b)$$ $$a^2 + 2ab + b^2 = (a + b)(a + b)$$ $$a^2 - 2ab + b^2 = (a - b)(a - b)$$ ✓ "Reverse FOIL": $x^2 + (b + a)x + ab = (x + a)(x + b)$
Example	***Factor this trinomial.*** $x^2 + 12x + 32 =$ **Solution:** Break the expression into groups: $(x^2 + 4x) + (8x + 32)$ Now factor out x from $x^2 + 4x : x(x + 4)$, and factor out 8 from $8x + 32$: $8(x + 4)$ Then: $(x^2 + 4x) + (8x + 32) = x(x + 4) + 8(x + 4)$ Now factor out like term: $(x + 4) \rightarrow (x + 4)(x + 8)$

Your Turn!		
	1) $x^2 + 3x - 4 =$ ————	2) $x^2 + 4x - 12 =$ ————
	3) $x^2 + x - 12 =$ ————	4) $x^2 - 6x + 8 =$ ————
	5) $x^2 + 7x + 12 =$ ————	6) $x^2 + 12x + 32 =$ ————
	7) $x^2 + 13x + 30 =$ ————	8) $x^2 - x + 72 =$ ————

Find more at

bit.ly/38EpdJA

Topic	Factoring Trinomials – Answers
Notes	To factor trinomial, use of the following methods: ✓ "FOIL": $(x + a)(x + b) = x^2 + (b + a)x + ab$ ✓ "Difference of Squares": $$a^2 - b^2 = (a + b)(a - b)$$ $$a^2 + 2ab + b^2 = (a + b)(a + b)$$ $$a^2 - 2ab + b^2 = (a - b)(a - b)$$ ✓ "Reverse FOIL": $x^2 + (b + a)x + ab = (x + a)(x + b)$
Example	**Factor this trinomial.** $x^2 + 12x + 32 =$ **Solution:** Break the expression into groups: $(x^2 + 4x) + (8x + 32)$ Now factor out x from $x^2 + 4x$: $x(x + 4)$, and factor out 8 from $8x + 32$: $8(x + 4)$ Then: $(x^2 + 4x) + (8x + 32) = x(x + 4) + 8(x + 4)$ Now factor out like term: $(x + 4) \rightarrow (x + 4)(x + 8)$

Your Turn!	1) $x^2 + 3x - 4 =$ $(x + 4)(x - 1)$	2) $x^2 + 4x - 12 =$ $(x - 2)(x + 6)$
	3) $x^2 + x - 12 =$ $(x - 3)(x + 4)$	4) $x^2 - 6x + 8 =$ $(x - 2)(x - 4)$
Find more at bit.ly/38EpdJA	5) $x^2 + 7x + 12 =$ $(x + 3)(x + 4)$	6) $x^2 + 12x + 32 =$ $(x + 8)(x + 4)$
	7) $x^2 + 13x + 30 =$ $(x + 10)(x + 3)$	8) $x^2 - x - 72 =$ $(x - 9)(x + 8)$

Topic	The Pythagorean Theorem
Notes	✓ In any right triangle: $a^2 + b^2 = c^2$
Example	Right triangle ABC (not shown) has two legs of lengths 18 cm (AB) and 24 cm (AC). What is the length of the third side (BC)? **Solution:** Use Pythagorean Theorem: $a^2 + b^2 = c^2$ Then: $a^2 + b^2 = c^2 \rightarrow 18^2 + 24^2 = c^2 \rightarrow 324 + 576 = c^2$ $c^2 = 900 \rightarrow c = \sqrt{900} = 30\ cm$
Your Turn!	1) _____ 2) _____ 8, ?, 6 34, 16, ? 3) _____ 4) _____ 13, 5, ? 10, ?, 8

Find more at

bit.ly/37Jl08v

Topic	The Pythagorean Theorem – Answers
Notes	✓ In any right triangle: $a^2 + b^2 = c^2$
Example	Right triangle ABC (not shown) has two legs of lengths 18 cm (AB) and 24 cm (AC). What is the length of the third side (BC)? **Solution:** Use Pythagorean Theorem: $a^2 + b^2 = c^2$ Then: $a^2 + b^2 = c^2 \rightarrow 18^2 + 24^2 = c^2 \rightarrow 324 + 576 = c^2$ $c^2 = 900 \rightarrow c = \sqrt{900} = 30\ cm$

Your Turn!	
1) 10 8 ? 6	2) 30 34 16 ?
3) 12 13 5 ?	4) 6 10 ? 8

Find more at

bit.ly/37Jl08v

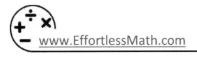

Topic	Triangles
Notes	✓ In any triangle the sum of all angles is 180 degrees. ✓ *0*Area of a triangle = $\frac{1}{2}$ $(base \times height)$
Example	**What is the area of the following triangle?** **Solution:** Use the area formula: Area $= \frac{1}{2}$ $(base \times height)$ $base = 16$ and $height = 6$ Area $= \frac{1}{2}(16 \times 6) = \frac{96}{2} = 48$

Your Turn!	
1) _____ 	2) _____
3) _____ 	4) _____

Find more at

bit.ly/3haZrRg

Topic	Triangles – Answers
Notes	✓ In any triangle the sum of all angles is 180 degrees. ✓ Area of a triangle = $\frac{1}{2}(base \times height)$
Example	*What is the area of the following triangle?* **Solution:** Use the area formula: Area $= \frac{1}{2}(base \times height)$ $base = 16$ and $height = 6$ Area $= \frac{1}{2}(16 \times 6) = \frac{96}{2} = 48$
Your Turn! **Find more at** bit.ly/3haZrRg	1) 120 20 ⊾ 12 3) 300 20 ⊾ 30
	2) 252 18 ⊾ 28 4) 680 34 ⊾ 40

Topic	Polygons
Notes	Perimeter of a square $= 4 \times side = 4s$ Perimeter of a rectangle $= 2(width + length)$ Perimeter of trapezoid $= a + b + c + d$ Perimeter of a regular hexagon $= 6a$ Perimeter of a parallelogram $= 2(l + w)$
Example	***Find the perimeter of following regular hexagon.*** **Solution:** Since the hexagon is regular, all sides are equal. Then: Perimeter of Hexagon $= 6 \times (one\ side)$ Perimeter of Hexagon $= 6 \times (one\ side) = 6 \times 9 = 54\ m$
Your Turn!	5) *(rectangle)* _____ 8 *in* 12 *in* 6) _____ 8 m 10 m 10 m 14 m
Find more at bit.ly/3nFNiGi	7) *(regular hexagon)* _____ 5 m 8) *(parallelogram)* _____ 9 *in* 11 *in*

Topic	Polygons – Answers
Notes	Perimeter of a square $= 4 \times side = 4s$ Perimeter of a rectangle $= 2(width + length)$ Perimeter of trapezoid $= a + b + c + d$ Perimeter of a regular hexagon $= 6a$ Perimeter of a parallelogram $= 2(l + w)$
Example	***Find the perimeter of following regular hexagon.*** **Solution:** Since the hexagon is regular, all sides are equal. Then: Perimeter of Hexagon $= 6 \times (one\ side)$ Perimeter of Hexagon $= 6 \times (one\ side) = 6 \times 9 = 54\ m$
Your Turn!	5) *(rectangle)* $40\ in$ **8 in** **12 in** 6) $42\ m$ $8\ m$ $10\ m$ $10\ m$ $14\ m$
Find more at bit.ly/3nFNiGi	7) *(regular hexagon)* $30\ m$ $5\ m$ 8) *(parallelogram)* $40\ in$ $9\ in$ $11\ in$

Topic	Circles
Notes	✓ In a circle, variable r is usually used for the radius and d for diameter and π is about 3.14. ✓ *Area of a circle* $= \pi r^2$ ✓ *Circumference of a circle* $= 2\pi r$
Example	**Find the area of the circle.** Solution: Use area formula: $Area = \pi r^2$ $r = 2\ in \rightarrow Area = \pi(2)^2 = 4\pi, \pi = 3.14$ **Then:** $Area = 4 \times 3.14 = 12.56\ in^2$

Your Turn!

Find the area of each circle. ($\pi = 3.14$)

1) _____ 5 cm

2) _____ 10 in

Find the Circumference of each circle. ($\pi = 3.14$)

3) _____ 8 cm

4) _____ 7 m

Topic	Circles – Answers
Notes	✓ In a circle, variable r is usually used for the radius and d for diameter and π is about 3.14. ✓ *Area of a circle = πr^2* ✓ *Circumference of a circle = $2\pi r$* r
Example	**Find the area of the circle.** **Solution:** Use area formula: $Area = \pi r^2$ $r = 2\ in \rightarrow Area = \pi(2)^2 = 4\pi,\ \pi = 3.14$ **Then:** $Area = 4 \times 3.14 = 12.56\ in^2$ $2\ in$
Your Turn!	**Find the area of each circle.** ($\pi = 3.14$)

Find the area of each circle. ($\pi = 3.14$)

1) $78.5 cm^2$

5 cm

2) $314\ in^2$

10 in

Find the Circumference of each circle. ($\pi = 3.14$)

3) $50.24\ cm$

8 cm

4) $43.96\ m$

7 m

Find more at

bit.ly/3nJdOP2

Topic	Cubes
Notes	✓ A cube is a three-dimensional solid object bounded by six square sides. ✓ Volume is the measure of the amount of space inside of a solid figure, like a cube, ball, cylinder or pyramid. ✓ Volume of a cube $= (one\ side)^3$ ✓ surface area of cube $= 6 \times (one\ side)^2$
Example	**Find the volume and surface area of the following cube.** 15 cm **Solution:** Use volume formula: $volume = (one\ side)^3$ Then: $volume = (one\ side)^3 = (15)^3 = 3,375\ cm^3$ Use surface area formula: $surface\ area\ of\ cube: 6(one\ side)^2 = 6(15)^2 = 6(225) = 1,350\ cm^2$
Your Turn!	**Find the volume of each cube.**
	1) _____ 9 in 2) _____ 13 ft
Find more at bit.ly/2M6PfOl	3) _____ 14 cm 4) _____ 20 m

Topic	Cubes – Answers
Notes	✓ A cube is a three-dimensional solid object bounded by six square sides. ✓ Volume is the measure of the amount of space inside of a solid figure, like a cube, ball, cylinder or pyramid. ✓ Volume of a cube $= (one\ side)^3$ ✓ surface area of cube $= 6 \times (one\ side)^2$
Example	***Find the volume and surface area of the following cube.*** 15 cm **Solution:** Use volume formula: $volume = (one\ side)^3$ Then: $volume = (one\ side)^3 = (15)^3 = 3{,}375\ cm^3$ Use surface area formula: $surface\ area\ of\ cube: 6(one\ side)^2 = 6(15)^2 = 6(225) = 1{,}350\ cm^2$
Your Turn! **Find more at** bit.ly/2M6PfOl	***Find the volume of each cube.*** 1) $729\ in^3$ 9 in 2) $2{,}197\ ft^3$ 13 ft 3) $2{,}744\ cm^3$ 14 cm 4) $8{,}000\ m^3$ 20 m

www.EffortlessMath.com

Topic	Trapezoids
Notes	✓ A quadrilateral with at least one pair of parallel sides is a trapezoid. ✓ Area of a trapezoid $= \frac{1}{2}h(b_1 + b_2)$
Example	*Calculate the area of the trapezoid.* Solution: Use area formula: $A = \frac{1}{2}h(b_1 + b_2)$ $b_1 = 8\ cm$, $b_2 = 12\ cm$ and $h = 14\ cm$ Then: $A = \frac{1}{2}(14)(12 + 8) = 7(20) = 140\ cm^2$

Your Turn!

1) _____

7 cm

4 cm

10 cm

2) _____

8 m

10 m

12 m

3) _____

7 ft

6 ft

15 ft

4) _____

8 cm

6 cm

12 cm

Find more at

bit.ly/3hpKACJ

Topic	Trapezoids – Answers
Notes	✓ A quadrilateral with at least one pair of parallel sides is a trapezoid. ✓ Area of a trapezoid $= \frac{1}{2}h(b_1 + b_2)$ *(diagram of trapezoid with b_2 on top, h inside, b_1 on bottom)*
Example	*Calculate the area of the trapezoid.* **Solution:** Use area formula: $A = \frac{1}{2}h(b_1 + b_2)$ $b_1 = 8\ cm$, $b_2 = 12\ cm$ and $h = 14\ cm$ Then: $A = \frac{1}{2}(14)(12 + 8) = 7(20) = 140\ cm^2$ *(diagram: 12 cm top, 14 cm inside, 8 cm bottom)*
Your Turn! **Find more at** bit.ly/3hpKACJ	1) $34\ cm^2$ *(diagram: 7 cm top, 4 cm left, 10 cm bottom)* 2) $100\ m^2$ *(diagram: 8 m top, 10 m height, 12 m bottom)* 3) $66\ ft^2$ *(diagram: 7 ft top, 6 ft height, 15 ft bottom)* 4) $60\ cm^2$ *(diagram: 8 cm top, 6 cm height, 12 cm bottom)*

Topic	**Rectangular Prisms**
Notes	✓ A solid 3-dimensional object which has six rectangular faces. ✓ Volume of a Rectangular prism = **Length × Width × Height** $Volume = l \times w \times h$ $Surface\ area = 2(wh + lw + lh)$
Example	**Find the volume and surface area of rectangular prism.** **Solution:** Use volume formula: $Volume = l \times w \times h$ Then: $Volume = 4 \times 2 \times 6 = 48\ m^3$ Use surface area formula: $Surface\ area = 2(wh + lw + lh)$ Then: $Surface\ area = 2\big((2 \times 6) + (4 \times 2) + (4 \times 6)\big)$ $= 2(12 + 8 + 24) = 2(44) = 88\ m^2$
Your Turn!	**Find the surface area of each Rectangular Prism.**

1) _____

5 ft
10 ft
3 ft

2) _____

8 cm
16 cm
6 cm

3) _____

12 m
18 m
10 m

4) _____

18 in
16 in
12 in

Topic	**Rectangular Prisms - Answers**
Notes	✓ A solid 3-dimensional object which has six rectangular faces. ✓ Volume of a Rectangular prism = **Length × Width × Height** $Volume = l \times w \times h$ $Surface\ area = 2(wh + lw + lh)$

Example

Find the volume and surface area of rectangular prism.
Solution:
 Use volume formula: $Volume = l \times w \times h$

Then: $Volume = 4 \times 2 \times 6 = 48\ m^3$

Use surface area formula: $Surface\ area = 2(wh + lw + lh)$

Then: $Surface\ area = 2\big((2 \times 6) + (4 \times 2) + (4 \times 6)\big)$

$= 2(12 + 8 + 24) = 2(44) = 88\ m^2$

(Figure: rectangular prism labeled 4 m, 6 m, 2 m)

Your Turn!

Find the surface area of each Rectangular Prism.

1) $190\ ft^2$

(Figure: 5 ft, 10 ft, 3 ft)

2) $544\ cm^2$

(Figure: 8 cm, 16 cm, 6 cm)

3) $1,032\ m^2$

(Figure: 12 m, 18 m, 10 m)

4) $1,392\ in^2$

(Figure: 18 in, 16 in, 12 in)

Find more at

bit.ly/3nKm2GT

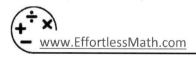

Topic	Cylinder
Notes	✓ A cylinder is a solid geometric figure with straight parallel sides and a circular or oval cross section. ✓ *Volume of Cylinder Formula* $= \pi(radius)^2 \times height$ $\pi = 3.14$ ✓ *Surface area of a cylinder* $= 2\pi r^2 + 2\pi rh$ *height* *radius*
Example	**Find the volume and Surface area of the follow Cylinder.** Solution: Use volume formula: $Volume = \pi(radius)^2 \times height$ Then: $Volume = \pi(3)^2 \times 12 = 9\pi \times 12 = 108\pi$ $\pi = 3.14$ **then:** $Volume = 108\pi = 339.12 \ cm^3$ Use surface area formula: $Surface \ area = 2\pi r^2 + 2\pi rh$ **Then:** $2\pi(3)^2 + 2\pi(3)(12) = 2\pi(9) + 2\pi(36) = 18\pi + 72\pi = 90\pi$ $\pi = 3.14$ **Then:** $Surface \ area = 90 \times 3.14 = 282.6 \ cm^2$ *12 cm* *3 cm*
Your Turn!	**Find the volume of each Cylinder.** ($\pi = 3.14$) 1) _____ *8 in* *3 in* 2) _____ *14 m* *5 m* **Find the Surface area of each Cylinder.** ($\pi = 3.14$) 3) _____ *15 ft* *9 ft* 4) _____ *12 cm* *6 cm*

Topic	Cylinder – Answers
Notes	✓ A cylinder is a solid geometric figure with straight parallel sides and a circular or oval cross section. ✓ $Volume\ of\ Cylinder\ Formula = \pi(radius)^2 \times height\ \ \pi = 3.14$ ✓ $Surface\ area\ of\ a\ cylinder = 2\pi r^2 + 2\pi rh$ *(diagram of cylinder labeled height and radius)*
Example	**Find the volume and Surface area of the follow Cylinder.** **Solution:** Use volume formula: $Volume = \pi(radius)^2 \times height$ Then: $Volume = \pi(3)^2 \times 12 = 9\pi \times 12 = 108\pi$ $\pi = 3.14$ **then:** $Volume = 108\pi = 339.12\ cm^3$ Use surface area formula: $Surface\ area = 2\pi r^2 + 2\pi rh$ **Then:** $2\pi(3)^2 + 2\pi(3)(12) = 2\pi(9) + 2\pi(36) = 18\pi + 72\pi = 90\pi$ $\pi = 3.14$ **Then:** $Surface\ area = 90 \times 3.14 = 282.6\ cm^2$ *(diagram of cylinder: 12 cm height, 3 cm radius)*
Your Turn! **Find more at** bit.ly/37LtcVM 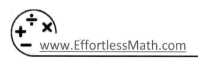	**Find the volume of each Cylinder.** ($\pi = 3.14$) 1) $226.08\ in^3$ *(cylinder: 8 in, 3 in)* 2) $1,099\ m^3$ *(cylinder: 14 m, 5 m)* **Find the Surface area of each Cylinder.** ($\pi = 3.14$) 3) $1,356.48\ ft^2$ *(cylinder: 15 ft, 9 ft)* 4) $678.24\ cm^2$ *(cylinder: 12 cm, 6 cm)*

Topic	Mean, Median, Mode, and Range of the Given Data
Notes	✓ Mean: $\dfrac{sum\ of\ the\ data}{total\ number\ of\ data\ entires}$ ✓ Mode: value in the list that appears most often. ✓ Median: is the middle number of a group of numbers that have been arranged in order by size. ✓ Range: the difference of largest value and smallest value in the list.
Example	**Find the mode and median of these numbers?** $16, 10, 6, 3, 1, 16, 2, 4$ **Solution:** Mode: value in the list that appears most often. Number 16 is the value in the list that appears most often (there are two number 16). To find median, write the numbers in order: $1, 2, 3, 4, 6, 10, 16, 16$ Number 4 and 6 are in the middle. Find their average: $\dfrac{4+6}{2} = \dfrac{10}{2} = 5$ The median is 5.
Your Turn! **Find more at** bit.ly/2KO86gg	1) $5, 2, 4, 8, 5, 6$ Mode: _____ Range: _____ Mean: _____ Median: _____ --- 3) $5, 4, 3, 2, 9, 5, 6, 8, 12$ Mode: _____ Range: _____ Mean: _____ Median: _____ ‖ 2) $6, 3, 2, 9, 5, 7, 2, 14$ Mode: _____ Range: _____ Mean: _____ Median: _____ --- 4) $10, 3, 8, 3, 9, 3, 4, 14$ Mode: _____ Range: _____ Mean: _____ Median: _____

Topic	Mean, Median, Mode, and Range of the Given Data - Answers
Notes	✓ Mean: $\dfrac{sum\ of\ the\ data}{total\ number\ of\ data\ entires}$ ✓ Mode: value in the list that appears most often. ✓ Median: is the middle number of a group of numbers that have been arranged in order by size. ✓ Range: the difference of largest value and smallest value in the list.
Example	***Find the mode and median of these numbers?*** $16, 10, 6, 3, 1, 16, 2, 4$ **Solution:** Mode: value in the list that appears most often. Number 16 is the value in the list that appears most often (there are two number 16). To find median, write the numbers in order: $1, 2, 3, 4, 6, 10, 16, 16$ Number 4 and 6 are in the middle. Find their average: $\dfrac{4+6}{2} = \dfrac{10}{2} = 5$ The median is 5.

Your Turn!		
	1) $5, 2, 4, 8, 5, 6$ Mode: 5 Range: 6 Mean: 5 Median: 5	**2)** $6, 3, 2, 9, 5, 7, 2, 14$ Mode: 2 Range: 12 Mean: 6 Median: 5.5
Find more at bit.ly/2KO86gg 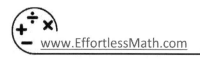	**3)** $5, 4, 3, 2, 9, 5, 6, 8, 12$ Mode: 5 Range: 10 Mean: 6 Median: 5	**4)** $10, 3, 8, 3, 9, 3, 4, 14$ Mode: 3 Range: 11 Mean: 6.75 Median: 6

Topic	**Probability Problems**
Notes	✓ Probability is the likelihood of something happening in the future. It is expressed as a number between zero (can never happen) to 1 (will always happen). ✓ Probability can be expressed as a fraction, a decimal, or a percent. ✓ Probability formula: $Probability = \frac{number\ of\ desired\ outcomes}{number\ of\ total\ outcomes}$
Example	**If there are 3 green balls, 4 red balls, and 10 blue balls in a basket, what is the probability that Jason will pick out a red ball from the basket?** **Solution:** There are 4 red ball and 17 are total number of balls. Therefore, probability that Jason will pick out a red ball from the basket is 4 out of 17 or $\frac{4}{3+4+10} = \frac{4}{17}$
Your Turn! **Find more at** bit.ly/3phwk1p	1) A number is chosen at random from 1 to 15. Find the probability of selecting a prime number. (A prime number is a whole number that is only divisible by itself and 1) _____
	2) There are only red and blue cards in a box. The probability of choosing a red card in the box at random is one third. If there are 24 blue cards, how many cards are in the box? _____
	3) A die is rolled, what is the probability that an odd number is obtained? _____

Topic	Probability Problems – Answers
Notes	✓ Probability is the likelihood of something happening in the future. It is expressed as a number between zero (can never happen) to 1 (will always happen). ✓ Probability can be expressed as a fraction, a decimal, or a percent. ✓ Probability formula: $Probability = \frac{number\ of\ desired\ outcomes}{number\ of\ total\ outcomes}$
Example	***If there are 3 green balls, 4 red balls, and 10 blue balls in a basket, what is the probability that Jason will pick out a red ball from the basket?*** **Solution:** There are 4 red ball and 17 are total number of balls. Therefore, probability that Jason will pick out a red ball from the basket is 4 out of 17 or $\frac{4}{3+4+10} = \frac{4}{17}$
Your Turn! **Find more at** bit.ly/3phwk1p 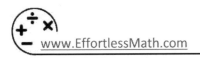	1) A number is chosen at random from 1 to 15. Find the probability of selecting a prime number. (A prime number is a whole number that is only divisible by itself and 1) $\frac{6}{15} = \frac{2}{5}$ *(There are 6 prime numbers from 1 to 15: 2, 3, 5, 7, 11, 13)*
	2) There are only red and blue cards in a box. The probability of choosing a red card in the box at random is one third. If there are 24 blue cards, how many cards are in the box? 36
	3) A die is rolled, what is the probability that an odd number is obtained? $\frac{1}{2}$

Topic	Pie Graph
Notes	✓ A Pie Chart is a circle chart divided into sectors, each sector represents the relative size of each value.
Example	A library has 460 books that include Mathematics, Physics, Chemistry, English and History. Use following graph to answer the question. **What is the number of Physics books?** **Solution:** Number of total books $= 460$ Percent of Physics books $= 25\% = 0.25$ Then, umber of Physics books: $$0.25 \times 460 = 115$$ History 10% · English 15% · Mathematics 30% · Chemistry 20% · Physics 25%
Your Turn!	The circle graph below shows all Mr. Smith's expenses for last month. Mr. Smith spent $400 for clothes last month. Foods 25% · Bills 20% · Others 23% · Clothes 20% · Books 12% Mr. Smith's last month expenses
Find more at bit.ly/34ECTDv	1) How much did Mr. Smith spend for his Books last month? _____ 2) How much did Mr. Smith spend for Bills last month? _____ 3) How much did Mr. Smith spend for his foods last month? _____

Topic	Pie Graph
Notes	✓ A Pie Chart is a circle chart divided into sectors, each sector represents the relative size of each value.
Example	A library has 460 books that include Mathematics, Physics, Chemistry, English and History. Use following graph to answer the question. **What is the number of Physics books?** **Solution:** Number of total books = 460 Percent of Physics books = 25% = 0.25 Then, umber of Physics books: $$0.25 \times 460 = 115$$ *History 10%, Mathematics 30%, English 15%, Chemistry 20%, Physics 25%*

Your Turn!	The circle graph below shows all Mr. Smith's expenses for last month. Mr. Smith spent $400 for clothes last month.
	Foods 25%, Bills 20%, Others 23%, Clothes 20%, Books 12% Mr. Smith's last month expenses
Find more at bit.ly/34ECTDv	1) How much did Mr. Smith spend for his Books last month? $240 2) How much did Mr. Smith spend for Bills last month? $400 3) How much did Mr. Smith spend for his foods last month? $500

Topic	**Permutations and Combinations**
Notes	✓ Permutations: The number of ways to choose a sample of k elements from a set of n distinct objects where order does matter, and replacements are not allowed. For a permutation problem, use this formula: $$_nP_k = \frac{n!}{(n-k)!}$$ ✓ Combination: The number of ways to choose a sample of r elements from a set of n distinct objects where order does not matter, and replacements are not allowed. For a combination problem, use this formula: $$_nC_r = \frac{n!}{r!\,(n-r)!}$$ ✓ Factorials are products, indicated by an exclamation mark. For example, 4! Equals: $4 \times 3 \times 2 \times 1$. Remember that 0! is defined to be equal to 1.
Example	*How many ways can we pick a team of 4 people from a group of 8?* **Solution:** Since the order doesn't matter, we need to use combination formula where n is 8 and r is 4. Then: $\frac{n!}{r!\,(n-r)!} = \frac{8!}{4!\,(8-4)!} = \frac{8!}{4!\,(4)!} = \frac{8\times7\times6\times5\times4!}{4!\,(4)!} = \frac{8\times7\times6\times5}{4\times3\times2\times1} = \frac{1{,}680}{24} = 70$
Your Turn! **Find more at** bit.ly/34BQgUY	1) In how many ways can 6 athletes be arranged in a straight line? _____
	2) How many ways can we award a first and second place prize among eight contestants? _____
	3) In how many ways can we choose 4 players from a team of 10 players? _____

Topic	Permutations and Combinations – Answers
Notes	✓ Permutations: The number of ways to choose a sample of k elements from a set of n distinct objects where order does matter, and replacements are not allowed. For a permutation problem, use this formula: $$_nP_k = \frac{n!}{(n-k)!}$$ ✓ Combination: The number of ways to choose a sample of r elements from a set of n distinct objects where order does not matter, and replacements are not allowed. For a combination problem, use this formula: $$_nC_r = \frac{n!}{r!\,(n-r)!}$$ ✓ Factorials are products, indicated by an exclamation mark. For example, 4! Equals: $4 \times 3 \times 2 \times 1$. Remember that 0! is defined to be equal to 1.
Example	***How many ways can we pick a team of 4 people from a group of 8?*** **Solution:** Since the order doesn't matter, we need to use combination formula where n is 8 and r is 4. Then: $\frac{n!}{r!\,(n-r)!} = \frac{8!}{4!\,(8-4)!} = \frac{8!}{4!\,(4)!} = \frac{8\times7\times6\times5\times4!}{4!\,(4)!} = \frac{8\times7\times6\times5}{4\times3\times2\times1} = \frac{1,680}{24} = 70$
Your Turn!	1) In how many ways can 6 athletes be arranged in a straight line? 720
	2) How many ways can we award a first and second place prize among eight contestants? 56
Find more at bit.ly/34BQgUY	3) In how many ways can we choose 4 players from a team of 10 players? 210

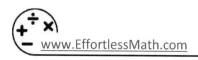

Topic	Function Notation and Evaluation
Notes	✓ Functions are mathematical operations that assign unique outputs to given inputs. ✓ Function notation is the way a function is written. It is meant to be a precise way of giving information about the function without a rather lengthy written explanation. ✓ The most popular function notation is $f(x)$ which is read "f of x". ✓ To evaluate a function, plug in the input (the given value or expression) for the function's variable (place holder, x).
Example	**Evaluate**: $h(n) = 2n^2 - 2$, find $h(2)$. **Solution:** Substitute n with 2: Then: $h(n) = 2n^2 - 2 \rightarrow h(2) = 2(2)^2 - 2 = 8 - 2 \rightarrow h(2) = 6$

Your Turn!	1) $f(x) = x - 1$, find $f(-2)$ _____	2) $g(x) = 3x + 2$, find $g(2)$ _____
	3) $g(n) = 2n - 8$, find $g(-1)$ _____	4) $h(n) = n^2 - 1$, find $h(-2)$ _____
	5) $f(x) = x^2 + 12$, find $f(5)$ _____	6) $g(x) = 2x^2 - 9$, find $g(-2)$ _____
Find more at bit.ly/3mls7lF	7) $w(x) = 3x^2 - x$, find $w(2n)$ _____	8) $p(x) = 2x^3 - 8$, find $p(-2a)$ _____

Topic	Function Notation and Evaluation – Answers
Notes	✓ Functions are mathematical operations that assign unique outputs to given inputs. ✓ Function notation is the way a function is written. It is meant to be a precise way of giving information about the function without a rather lengthy written explanation. ✓ The most popular function notation is $f(x)$ which is read "f of x". ✓ To evaluate a function, plug in the input (the given value or expression) for the function's variable (place holder, x).
Example	**Evaluate**: $h(n) = 2n^2 - 2$, find $h(2)$. **Solution:** Substitute n with 2: Then: $h(n) = 2n^2 - 2 \rightarrow h(2) = 2(2)^2 - 2 = 8 - 2 \rightarrow h(2) = 6$

Your Turn!		
Find more at bit.ly/3mls7lF	1) $f(x) = x - 1$, find $f(-2)$ $f(-2) = -3$	2) $g(x) = 3x + 2$, find $g(2)$ $g(2) = 8$
	3) $g(n) = 2n - 8$, find $g(-1)$ $g(-1) = -10$	4) $h(n) = n^2 - 1$, find $h(-2)$ $h(-2) = 3$
	5) $f(x) = x^2 + 12$, find $f(5)$ $f(5) = 37$	6) $g(x) = 2x^2 - 9$, find $g(-2)$ $g(-2) = -1$
	7) $w(x) = 3x^2 - x$, find $w(2n)$ $w(3n) = 12n^2 - 2n$	8) $p(x) = 2x^3 - 8$, find $p(-2a)$ $p(-2a) = -16a^3 - 8$

Topic	Adding and Subtracting Functions
Notes	✓ Just like we can add and subtract numbers and expressions, we can add or subtract two functions and simplify or evaluate them. The result is a new function. ✓ For two functions $f(x)$ and $g(x)$, we can create two new functions: $(f+g)(x) = f(x) + g(x)$ and $(f-g)(x) = f(x) - g(x)$
Example	$g(a) = 2a - 5$, $f(a) = a + 8$, Find: $(g+f)(a)$ **Solution:** $(g+f)(a) = g(a) + f(a)$ Then: $(g+f)(a) = (2a-5) + (a+8) = 3a+3$

Your Turn!		
	1) $g(x) = x - 3$ $h(x) = 2x + 5$ Find: $(h+g)(2)$ _____	2) $f(x) = 2x + 6$ $g(x) = -x - 5$ Find: $(f+g)(3)$ _____
	3) $f(x) = 5x + 8$ $g(x) = 3x - 12$ Find: $(f-g)(-2)$ _____	4) $h(x) = 2x^2 - 10$ $g(x) = 3x + 12$ Find: $(h+g)(3)$ _____
Find more at bit.ly/3hdeFVO	5) $g(x) = 10x - 7$ $h(x) = 3x^2 + 11$ Find: $(h-g)(x)$ _____	6) $h(x) = -x^2 - 15$ $g(x) = 3x^2 + 18$ Find: $(h-g)(a)$ _____

Topic	Adding and Subtracting Functions – Answers
Notes	✓ Just like we can add and subtract numbers and expressions, we can add or subtract two functions and simplify or evaluate them. The result is a new function. ✓ For two functions $f(x)$ and $g(x)$, we can create two new functions: $(f + g)(x) = f(x) + g(x)$ and $(f - g)(x) = f(x) - g(x)$
Example	$g(a) = 2a - 5, f(a) = a + 8$, Find: $(g + f)(a)$ **Solution:** $(g + f)(a) = g(a) + f(a)$ Then: $(g + f)(a) = (2a - 5) + (a + 8) = 3a + 3$

Your Turn!		
	1) $g(x) = x - 3$ $h(x) = 2x + 5$ Find: $(h + g)(2)$ 8	2) $f(x) = 2x + 6$ $g(x) = -x - 5$ Find: $(f + g)(3)$ 4
	3) $f(x) = 5x + 8$ $g(x) = 3x - 12$ Find: $(f - g)(-2)$ 16	4) $h(x) = 2x^2 - 10$ $g(x) = 3x + 12$ Find: $(h + g)(3)$ 29
Find more at bit.ly/3hdeFVO	5) $g(x) = 10x - 7$ $h(x) = 3x^2 + 11$ Find: $(h - g)(x)$ $3x^2 - 10x + 18$	6) $h(x) = -x^2 - 15$ $g(x) = 3x^2 + 18$ Find: $(h - g)(a)$ $-4a^2 - 33$

Topic	**Multiplying and Dividing Functions**
Notes	✓ Just like we can multiply and divide numbers and expressions, we can multiply and divide two functions and simplify or evaluate them. ✓ For two functions $f(x)$ and $g(x)$, we can create two new functions: $(f.g)(x) = f(x).g(x)$ and $\left(\frac{f}{g}\right)(x) = \frac{f(x)}{g(x)}$
Example	$g(x) = x + 5, f(x) = x - 3$, Find: $(g.f)(2)$ **Solution:** $(g.f)(x) = g(x).f(x) = (x+5)(x-3) = x^2 - 3x + 5x - 15 = x^2 + 2x - 15$ Substitute x with 2: $(g.f)(x) = (2)^2 + 2(2) - 15 = 4 + 4 - 15 = -7$

Your Turn!	1) $g(x) = x - 1$ $h(x) = x + 2$ Find: $(g.h)(-3)$ ————	2) $f(x) = x + 2$ $g(x) = -x - 3$ Find: $\left(\frac{f}{g}\right)(-4)$ ————
	3) $f(x) = 5x + 3$ $g(x) = 2x - 4$ Find: $\left(\frac{f}{g}\right)(5)$ ————	4) $h(x) = x^2 - 2$ $g(x) = x + 4$ Find: $(g.h)(3)$ ————
Find more at bit.ly/3ph7kHA	5) $g(x) = 2x - 8$ $h(x) = x^2 + 6$ Find: $(g.h)(-2)$ ————	6) $h(x) = 3x^2 - 8$ $g(x) = 4x + 3$ Find: $\left(\frac{h}{g}\right)(-1)$ ————

Topic	Multiplying and Dividing Functions - Answers
Notes	✓ Just like we can multiply and divide numbers and expressions, we can multiply and divide two functions and simplify or evaluate them. ✓ For two functions $f(x)$ and $g(x)$, we can create two new functions: $$(f \cdot g)(x) = f(x) \cdot g(x) \text{ and } \left(\frac{f}{g}\right)(x) = \frac{f(x)}{g(x)}$$
Example	$g(x) = x + 5, f(x) = x - 3$, Find: $(g \cdot f)(2)$ **Solution:** $(g \cdot f)(x) = g(x) \cdot f(x) = (x + 5)(x - 3) = x^2 - 3x + 5x - 15 = x^2 + 2x - 15$ Substitute x with 2: $(g \cdot f)(x) = (2)^2 + 2(2) - 15 = 4 + 4 - 15 = -7$

Your Turn!		
	1) $g(x) = x - 1$ $h(x) = x + 2$ Find: $(g \cdot h)(-3)$ $(g \cdot h)(-3) = 4$	2) $f(x) = x + 2$ $g(x) = -x - 3$ Find: $\left(\frac{f}{g}\right)(-4)$ $\left(\frac{f}{g}\right)(-4) = -2$
	3) $f(x) = 5x + 3$ $g(x) = 2x - 4$ Find: $\left(\frac{f}{g}\right)(5)$ $\left(\frac{f}{g}\right)(5) = \frac{14}{3}$	4) $h(x) = x^2 - 2$ $g(x) = x + 4$ Find: $(g \cdot h)(3)$ $(g \cdot h)(3) = 49$
Find more at bit.ly/3ph7kHA 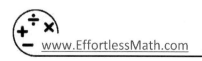	5) $g(x) = 2x - 8$ $h(x) = x^2 + 6$ Find: $(g \cdot h)(-2)$ $(g \cdot h)(-2) = -120$	6) $h(x) = 3x^2 - 8$ $g(x) = 4x + 3$ Find: $\left(\frac{h}{g}\right)(-1)$ $\left(\frac{h}{g}\right)(-1) = 5$

Topic	Composition of Functions
Notes	✓ "Composition of functions" simply means combining two or more functions in a way where the output from one function becomes the input for the next function. ✓ The notation used for composition is: $(f o g)(x) = f(g(x))$ and is read "f composed with g of x" or "f of g of x".
Example	*Using $f(x) = x - 8$ and $g(x) = x + 2$, find:* $(f o g)(3)$ **Solution:** $(f o g)(x) = f(g(x))$ *Then:* $(f o g)(x) = f(g(x)) = f(x + 2) = x + 2 - 8 = x - 6$ Substitute x with 3: $(f o g)(3) = f(g(3)) = 3 - 6 = -3$
Your Turn!	1) $f(x) = 3x$ $g(x) = x + 2$ Find: $(fog)(2)$ ___ 2) $f(x) = x + 3$ $g(x) = x - 1$ Find: $(fog)(-2)$ ___
	3) $f(x) = 3x$ $g(x) = x + 4$ Find: $(gof)(4)$ ___ 4) $h(x) = 2x - 2$ $g(x) = x + 4$ Find: $(goh)(2)$ ___
Find more at bit.ly/2WHBkAg	5) $f(x) = 3x - 1$ $g(x) = x + 8$ Find: $(fog)(-1)$ ___ 6) $f(x) = x^2 - 4$ $g(x) = 3x + 1$ Find: $(gof)(2)$ ___

Topic	Composition of Functions – Answers
Notes	✓ "Composition of functions" simply means combining two or more functions in a way where the output from one function becomes the input for the next function. ✓ The notation used for composition is: $(f \circ g)(x) = f(g(x))$ and is read "f composed with g of x" or "f of g of x".
Example	*Using* $f(x) = x - 8$ *and* $g(x) = x + 2$, *find:* $(f \circ g)(3)$ **Solution:** $(f \circ g)(x) = f(g(x))$ *Then:* $(f \circ g)(x) = f(g(x)) = f(x + 2) = x + 2 - 8 = x - 6$ Substitute x with 3: $(f \circ g)(3) = f(g(3)) = 3 - 6 = -3$

Your Turn!

1) $f(x) = 3x$
$g(x) = x + 2$
Find: $(f \circ g)(2)$
12

2) $f(x) = x + 3$
$g(x) = x - 1$
Find: $(f \circ g)(-2)$
0

3) $f(x) = 3x$
$g(x) = x + 4$
Find: $(g \circ f)(4)$
16

4) $h(x) = 2x - 2$
$g(x) = x + 4$
Find: $(g \circ h)(2)$
6

5) $f(x) = 3x - 1$
$g(x) = x + 8$
Find: $(f \circ g)(-1)$
20

6) $f(x) = x^2 - 4$
$g(x) = 3x + 1$
Find: $(g \circ f)(2)$
1

Time to Test

Time to refine your skill with a practice examination

Take practice FTCE Math Tests to simulate the test day experience. After you've finished, score your tests using the answer keys.

Before You Start

- You'll need a pencil, a calculator and a timer to take the test.

- For each question, there are four possible answers. Choose which one is best.

- It's okay to guess. There is no penalty for wrong answers.

- Use the answer sheet provided to record your answers.

- The FTCE Mathematics test contains a formula sheet, which displays formulas relating to geometric measurement and certain algebra concepts. Formulas are provided to test-takers so that they may focus on application, rather than the memorization, of formulas.

- After you've finished the test, review the answer key to see where you went wrong.

Good Luck!

FTCE General Knowledge Math

Practice Test 1

2022-2023

Total number of questions: 45

Total time: 100 Minutes

Basic Calculator is permitted for FTCE General Knowledge Math Test.

FTCE Math Practice Test Answer Sheet

Remove (or photocopy) this answer sheet and use it to complete the practice test.

FTCE Math Practice Test 1		
1 Ⓐ Ⓑ Ⓒ Ⓓ	16 Ⓐ Ⓑ Ⓒ Ⓓ	31 Ⓐ Ⓑ Ⓒ Ⓓ
2 Ⓐ Ⓑ Ⓒ Ⓓ	17 Ⓐ Ⓑ Ⓒ Ⓓ	32 Ⓐ Ⓑ Ⓒ Ⓓ
3 Ⓐ Ⓑ Ⓒ Ⓓ	18 Ⓐ Ⓑ Ⓒ Ⓓ	33 Ⓐ Ⓑ Ⓒ Ⓓ
4 Ⓐ Ⓑ Ⓒ Ⓓ	19 Ⓐ Ⓑ Ⓒ Ⓓ	34 Ⓐ Ⓑ Ⓒ Ⓓ
5 Ⓐ Ⓑ Ⓒ Ⓓ	20 Ⓐ Ⓑ Ⓒ Ⓓ	35 Ⓐ Ⓑ Ⓒ Ⓓ
6 Ⓐ Ⓑ Ⓒ Ⓓ	21 Ⓐ Ⓑ Ⓒ Ⓓ	36 Ⓐ Ⓑ Ⓒ Ⓓ
7 Ⓐ Ⓑ Ⓒ Ⓓ	22 Ⓐ Ⓑ Ⓒ Ⓓ	37 Ⓐ Ⓑ Ⓒ Ⓓ
8 Ⓐ Ⓑ Ⓒ Ⓓ	23 Ⓐ Ⓑ Ⓒ Ⓓ	38 Ⓐ Ⓑ Ⓒ Ⓓ
9 Ⓐ Ⓑ Ⓒ Ⓓ	24 Ⓐ Ⓑ Ⓒ Ⓓ	39 Ⓐ Ⓑ Ⓒ Ⓓ
10 Ⓐ Ⓑ Ⓒ Ⓓ	25 Ⓐ Ⓑ Ⓒ Ⓓ	40 Ⓐ Ⓑ Ⓒ Ⓓ
11 Ⓐ Ⓑ Ⓒ Ⓓ	26 Ⓐ Ⓑ Ⓒ Ⓓ	41 Ⓐ Ⓑ Ⓒ Ⓓ
12 Ⓐ Ⓑ Ⓒ Ⓓ	27 Ⓐ Ⓑ Ⓒ Ⓓ	42 Ⓐ Ⓑ Ⓒ Ⓓ
13 Ⓐ Ⓑ Ⓒ Ⓓ	28 Ⓐ Ⓑ Ⓒ Ⓓ	43 Ⓐ Ⓑ Ⓒ Ⓓ
14 Ⓐ Ⓑ Ⓒ Ⓓ	29 Ⓐ Ⓑ Ⓒ Ⓓ	44 Ⓐ Ⓑ Ⓒ Ⓓ
15 Ⓐ Ⓑ Ⓒ Ⓓ	30 Ⓐ Ⓑ Ⓒ Ⓓ	45 Ⓐ Ⓑ Ⓒ Ⓓ

Mathematics Reference Sheet

Area

	Triangle	$A = \dfrac{1}{2}bh$
	Rectangle	$A = \ell w$
	Trapezoid	$A = \dfrac{1}{2}h(b_1 + b_2)$
	Parallelogram	$A = bh$
	Circle	$A = \pi r^2$

KEY	
b = base	d = diameter
h = height	r = radius
ℓ = length	A = area
w = width	C = circumference
$S.A.$ = surface area	V = volume
	B = area of base
Use 3.14 or $\dfrac{22}{7}$ for π	

Circumference
$$C = \pi d = 2\pi r$$

Surface Area
1. Surface area of a prism or pyramid equals the sum of the areas of all faces.

2. Surface area of a cylinder equals the sum of the areas of the bases and the area of its rectangular wrap.

$$S.A. = 2(\pi r^2) + 2(\pi r)h$$

3. Surface area of a sphere: $S.A. = 4\pi r^2$

Volume
1. Volume of a prism or cylinder equals the <u>Area of the Base</u> (B) times the height (h).
$V = Bh$

2. Volume of a pyramid or cone equals $\dfrac{1}{3}$ times the <u>Area of the Base</u> (B) times the height (h).

$$V = \dfrac{1}{3}Bh$$

3. Volume of a sphere: $V = \dfrac{4}{3}\pi r^3$

Pythagorean theorem: $a^2 + b^2 = c^2$

Simple interest formula: $I = prt$

I = simple interest, p = principal,
r = rate, t = time.

Distance formula: $d = rt$

d = distance, r = rate, t = time.

Given a line containing points
(x_1, y_1) **and** (x_2, y_2)

- **Slope of line**

$$\frac{y_2 - y_1}{x_2 - x_1}$$

- **Distance between two points**

$$\sqrt{(x_2 - x_1)^2 + (y_2 - y_1)^2}$$

- **Midpoint between two points**

$$\left(\frac{x_1 + x_2}{2}, \frac{y_1 + y_2}{2} \right)$$

Conversions

1 yard = 3 feet = 36 inches
1 mile = 1,760 yards = 5,280 feet
1 acre = 43,560 square feet
1 hour = 60 minutes
1 minute = 60 seconds

1 cup = 8 fluid ounces
1 pint = 2 cups
1 quart = 2 pints
1 gallon = 4 quarts
1 pound = 16 ounces
1 ton = 2,000 pounds

1 liter = 1000 milliliters = 1000 cubic centimeters
1 meter = 100 centimeters = 1000 millimeters
1 kilometer = 1000 meters
1 gram = 1000 milligrams
1 kilogram = 1000 grams

Metric numbers with four digits are presented without a comma (e.g., 9960 kilometers).
For metric numbers greater than four digits, a space is used instead of a comma
(e.g., 12 500 liters).

1) The mean of 50 test scores was calculated as 90. But, it turned out that one of the scores was misread as 94 but it was 69. What is the mean?

   A. 85

   B. 87

   C. 89.5

   D. 90.5

2) Two dice are thrown simultaneously, what is the probability of getting a sum of 5 or 8?

   A. $\dfrac{1}{3}$

   B. $\dfrac{11}{36}$

   C. $\dfrac{1}{16}$

   D. $\dfrac{1}{4}$

3) Which of the following is equal to the expression below?

$$(5x + 2y)(2x - y)$$

   A. $4x^2 - 2y^2$

   B. $2x^2 + 6xy - 2y^2$

   C. $24x^2 + 2xy - 2y^2$

   D. $10x^2 - xy - 2y^2$

4) What is the product of all possible values of x in the following equation?

$$|x - 10| = 4$$

   A. 3

   B. 7

   C. 13

   D. 84

5) What is the slope of a line that is perpendicular to the line $4x - 2y = 6$?

   A. -2

   B. $-\frac{1}{2}$

   C. 4

   D. 12

6) What is the value of the expression $6(x - 2y) + (2 - x)^2$ when $x = 3$ and $y = -2$?

   A. -4

   B. 20

   C. 43

   D. 50

7) A swimming pool holds 2,500 cubic feet of water. The swimming pool is 25 feet long and 10 feet wide. How deep is the swimming pool?

   A. $2\,feet$

   B. $4\,feet$

   C. $6\,feet$

   D. $10\,feet$

8) Four one − foot rulers can be split among how many users to leave each with $\frac{1}{3}$ of a ruler?

   A. 4

   B. 6

   C. 12

   D. 24

9) What is the area of a square whose diagonal is 4?

   A. 4

   B. 8

   C. 16

   D. 64

10) The average of five numbers is 26. If a sixth number 42 is added, then, what is the new average? (round your answer to the nearest hundredth)

A. 25

B. 26.5

C. 27

D. 28.66

Questions 11 to 13 are based on the following data

The result of a research shows the number of men and women in four cities of a country.

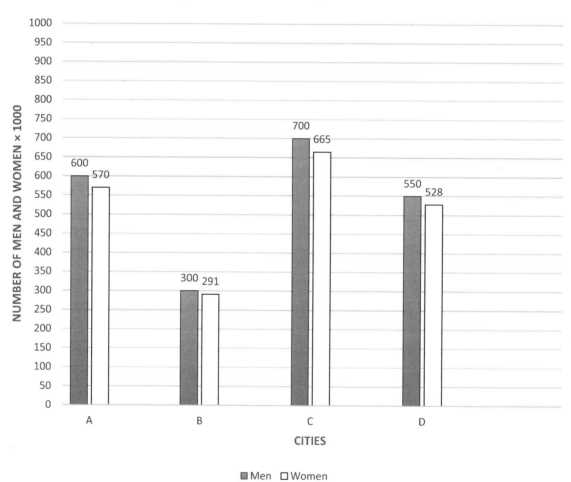

Number of men and women in four cities

11) What's the maximum ratio of the number of women to number of men in each city?

    A. 0.98

    B. 0.97

    C. 0.96

    D. 0.95

12) What's the ratio of the percentage of men in city A to percentage of women in city C?

    A. $\dfrac{10}{9}$

    B. $\dfrac{9}{10}$

    C. 1

    D. $\dfrac{20}{19}$

13) How many women should be added to city D to change the ratio of women to men to 1.2?

    A. 130

    B. 129

    C. 132

    D. 131

14) Jason needs an 70% average in his writing class to pass. On his first 4 exams, he earned scores of 68%, 72%, 85%, and 90%. What is the minimum score Jason can earn on his fifth and final test to pass?

    A. 80%,

    B. 70%

    C. 68%

    D. 35%

15) What is the value of x in the following equation? $\dfrac{2}{3}x + \dfrac{1}{6} = \dfrac{1}{2}$

    A. 6

    B. $\dfrac{1}{2}$

    C. $\dfrac{1}{3}$

    D. $\dfrac{1}{4}$

16) A bank is offering 4.5% simple interest on a saving account. If you deposit $12,000, how much interest will you earn in two years?

    A. $420

    B. $1,080

    C. $4,200

    D. $8,400

17) Simplify $7x^2y^3(2x^2y)^3 =$

    A. $12x^4y^6$

    B. $12x^8y^6$

    C. $56x^4y^6$

    D. $56x^8y^6$

18) What is the surface area of the cylinder below?

    A. $40\ \pi\ in^2$

    B. $57\ \pi\ in^2$

    C. $66\ \pi\ in^2$

    D. $288\ \pi\ in^2$

19) Last week 25,000 fans attended a football match. This week three times as many bought tickets, but one sixth of them cancelled their tickets. How many are attending this week?

    A. 48,000

    B. 54,000

    C. 62,500

    D. 75,000

20) What is the perimeter of a square that has an area of 49 square inches?

    A. $144\ inches$

    B. $64\ inches$

    C. $56\ inches$

    D. $28\ inches$

21) If $f(x) = 2x^3 + 5x^2 + 2x$ and $g(x) = -4$, what is the value of $f(g(x))$?

 A. 56

 B. 32

 C. 24

 D. -56

22) A cruise line ship left Port A and traveled 50 miles due west and then 120 miles due north.

 At this point, what is the shortest distance from the cruise to port A?

 A. $70\ miles$

 B. $80\ miles$

 C. $150\ miles$

 D. $130\ miles$

23) What is the equivalent temperature of $104°F$ in Celsius?

$$C = \frac{5}{9}(F - 32)$$

 A. 32

 B. 40

 C. 48

 D. 52

24) The perimeter of a rectangular yard is 72 meters. What is its length if its width is twice its length?

 A. $12\ meters$

 B. $18\ meters$

 C. $20\ meters$

 D. $24\ meters$

25) The average of 6 numbers is 14. The average of 4 of those numbers is 10. What is the average of the other two numbers?

 A. 10

 B. 12

 C. 14

 D. 22

26) If 150% of a number is 75, then what is the 80% of that number?

    A. 40

    B. 50

    C. 70

    D. 85

27) What is the slope of the line: $4x - 2y = 12$

    A. -1

    B. -2

    C. 1

    D. 2

28) In two successive years, the population of a town is increased by 10% and 20%. What percent of the population is increased after two years?

    A. 30%

    B. 32%

    C. 35%

    D. 68%

29) The area of a circle is 36π. What is the diameter of the circle?

    A. 4

    B. 8

    C. 12

    D. 14

30) If 20% of a number is 4, what is the number?

    A. 4

    B. 8

    C. 10

    D. 20

31) If a tree casts a 26–foot shadow at the same time that a 3 feet yardstick casts a 2–foot shadow, what is the height of the tree?

   A. 24 *ft*

   B. 28 *ft*

   C. 39 *ft*

   D. 48 *ft*

32) Jason is 9 miles ahead of Joe running at 6.5 miles per hour and Joe is running at the speed of 8 miles per hour. How long does it take Joe to catch Jason?

   A. 3 *hours*

   B. 4 *hours*

   C. 6 *hours*

   D. 8 *hours*

33) 44 students took an exam and 11 of them failed. What percent of the students passed the exam?

   A. 20%

   B. 40%

   C. 60%

   D. 75%

34) If $f(x) = 2x^3 + 5x^2 + 2x$ and $g(x) = -3$, what is the value of $f(g(x))$?

   A. 36

   B. 32

   C. 24

   D. −15

35) The diagonal of a rectangle is 10 inches long and the height of the rectangle is 6 inches. What is the perimeter of the rectangle?

   A. 10 *inches*

   B. 12 *inches*

   C. 16 *inches*

   D. 28 *inches*

36) The perimeter of the trapezoid below is $40\ cm$. What is its area?

    A. $48\ cm^2$

    B. $98\ cm^2$

    C. $140\ cm^2$

    D. $576\ cm^2$

37) If $f(x)=2x^3+2$ and $(x)=\frac{1}{x}$, what is the value of $f(g(x))$?

    A. $\dfrac{1}{2x^3+2}$

    B. $\dfrac{2}{x^3}$

    C. $\dfrac{1}{2x}$

    D. $\dfrac{2}{x^3}+2$

38) A cruise line ship left Port A and traveled 80 miles due west and then 150 miles due north.

    At this point, what is the shortest distance from the cruise to port A?

    A. $70\ miles$

    B. $80\ miles$

    C. $150\ miles$

    D. $170\ miles$

39) If the ratio of $5a$ to $2b$ is $\frac{1}{10}$, what is the ratio of a to b?

    A. 10

    B. 25

    C. $\dfrac{1}{25}$

    D. $\dfrac{1}{20}$

40) If $x=9$, what is the value of y in the following equation? $2y=\dfrac{2x^2}{3}+6$

    A. 30

    B. 45

    C. 60

    D. 120

41) If $\frac{x-3}{5} = N$ and $N = 6$, what is the value of x?

   A. 25

   B. 28

   C. 30

   D. 33

42) Which of the following is equal to $b^{\frac{3}{5}}$?

   A. $\sqrt{b^{\frac{5}{3}}}$

   B. $b^{\frac{5}{3}}$

   C. $\sqrt[5]{b^3}$

   D. $\sqrt[3]{b^5}$

43) On Saturday, Sara read N pages of a book each hour for 3 hours, and Mary read M pages of a book each hour for 4 hours. Which of the following represents the total number of pages of book read by Sara and Mary on Saturday?

   A. $12MN$

   B. $3N + 4M$

   C. $7MN$

   D. $4N + 3M$

44) Sara opened a bank account that earns 2 percent compounded annually. Her initial deposit was \$150, and she uses the expression $\$150(x)^n$ to find the value of the account after n years. What is the value of x in the expression?

   A. 0.02

   B. 0.20

   C. 20%

   D. 1.02

45) If function is defined as $f(x) = bx^2 + 15$, and b is a constant and $f(2) = 35$. What is the value of $f(5)$?

   A. 25

   B. 35

   C. 140

   D. 165

End of FTCE Mathematics Practice Test 1

FTCE General Knowledge Math

Practice Test 2

2022–2023

Total number of questions: 45

Total time: 100 Minutes

Basic Calculator is permitted for FTCE General Knowledge Math Test.

FTCE Math Practice Test Answer Sheet

Remove (or photocopy) this answer sheet and use it to complete the practice test.

FTCE Math Practice Test 2		
1 Ⓐ Ⓑ Ⓒ Ⓓ	16 Ⓐ Ⓑ Ⓒ Ⓓ	31 Ⓐ Ⓑ Ⓒ Ⓓ
2 Ⓐ Ⓑ Ⓒ Ⓓ	17 Ⓐ Ⓑ Ⓒ Ⓓ	32 Ⓐ Ⓑ Ⓒ Ⓓ
3 Ⓐ Ⓑ Ⓒ Ⓓ	18 Ⓐ Ⓑ Ⓒ Ⓓ	33 Ⓐ Ⓑ Ⓒ Ⓓ
4 Ⓐ Ⓑ Ⓒ Ⓓ	19 Ⓐ Ⓑ Ⓒ Ⓓ	34 Ⓐ Ⓑ Ⓒ Ⓓ
5 Ⓐ Ⓑ Ⓒ Ⓓ	20 Ⓐ Ⓑ Ⓒ Ⓓ	35 Ⓐ Ⓑ Ⓒ Ⓓ
6 Ⓐ Ⓑ Ⓒ Ⓓ	21 Ⓐ Ⓑ Ⓒ Ⓓ	36 Ⓐ Ⓑ Ⓒ Ⓓ
7 Ⓐ Ⓑ Ⓒ Ⓓ	22 Ⓐ Ⓑ Ⓒ Ⓓ	37 Ⓐ Ⓑ Ⓒ Ⓓ
8 Ⓐ Ⓑ Ⓒ Ⓓ	23 Ⓐ Ⓑ Ⓒ Ⓓ	38 Ⓐ Ⓑ Ⓒ Ⓓ
9 Ⓐ Ⓑ Ⓒ Ⓓ	24 Ⓐ Ⓑ Ⓒ Ⓓ	39 Ⓐ Ⓑ Ⓒ Ⓓ
10 Ⓐ Ⓑ Ⓒ Ⓓ	25 Ⓐ Ⓑ Ⓒ Ⓓ	40 Ⓐ Ⓑ Ⓒ Ⓓ
11 Ⓐ Ⓑ Ⓒ Ⓓ	26 Ⓐ Ⓑ Ⓒ Ⓓ	41 Ⓐ Ⓑ Ⓒ Ⓓ
12 Ⓐ Ⓑ Ⓒ Ⓓ	27 Ⓐ Ⓑ Ⓒ Ⓓ	42 Ⓐ Ⓑ Ⓒ Ⓓ
13 Ⓐ Ⓑ Ⓒ Ⓓ	28 Ⓐ Ⓑ Ⓒ Ⓓ	43 Ⓐ Ⓑ Ⓒ Ⓓ
14 Ⓐ Ⓑ Ⓒ Ⓓ	29 Ⓐ Ⓑ Ⓒ Ⓓ	44 Ⓐ Ⓑ Ⓒ Ⓓ
15 Ⓐ Ⓑ Ⓒ Ⓓ	30 Ⓐ Ⓑ Ⓒ Ⓓ	45 Ⓐ Ⓑ Ⓒ Ⓓ

Mathematics Reference Sheet

Area

 Triangle $A = \dfrac{1}{2}bh$

Rectangle $A = \ell w$

Trapezoid $A = \dfrac{1}{2}h\,(b_1 + b_2)$

KEY	
b = base	d = diameter
h = height	r = radius
ℓ = length	A = area
w = width	C = circumference
S.A. = surface area	V = volume
	B = area of base

Parallelogram $A = bh$

Use 3.14 or $\dfrac{22}{7}$ for π

Circle $A = \pi r^2$

Circumference
$C = \pi d = 2\pi r$

Surface Area
1. Surface area of a prism or pyramid equals the sum of the areas of all faces.

2. Surface area of a cylinder equals the sum of the areas of the bases and the area of its rectangular wrap.

$S.A. = 2(\pi r^2) + 2(\pi r)h$

3. Surface area of a sphere: $S.A. = 4\pi r^2$

Volume
1. Volume of a prism or cylinder equals the <u>Area of the Base</u> (B) times the height (h).
   $V = Bh$

2. Volume of a pyramid or cone equals $\dfrac{1}{3}$ times the <u>Area of the Base</u> (B) times the height (h).

$V = \dfrac{1}{3}Bh$

3. Volume of a sphere: $V = \dfrac{4}{3}\pi r^3$

Pythagorean theorem: $a^2 + b^2 = c^2$

Simple interest formula: $I = prt$

I = simple interest, p = principal, r = rate, t = time.

Distance formula: $d = rt$

d = distance, r = rate, t = time.

Given a line containing points (x_1, y_1) and (x_2, y_2)

- **Slope of line**

$$\frac{y_2 - y_1}{x_2 - x_1}$$

- **Distance between two points**

$$\sqrt{(x_2 - x_1)^2 + (y_2 - y_1)^2}$$

- **Midpoint between two points**

$$\left(\frac{x_1 + x_2}{2}, \frac{y_1 + y_2}{2}\right)$$

Conversions

1 yard = 3 feet = 36 inches
1 mile = 1,760 yards = 5,280 feet
1 acre = 43,560 square feet
1 hour = 60 minutes
1 minute = 60 seconds

1 liter = 1000 milliliters = 1000 cubic centimeters
1 meter = 100 centimeters = 1000 millimeters
1 kilometer = 1000 meters
1 gram = 1000 milligrams
1 kilogram = 1000 grams

1 cup = 8 fluid ounces
1 pint = 2 cups
1 quart = 2 pints
1 gallon = 4 quarts
1 pound = 16 ounces
1 ton = 2,000 pounds

Metric numbers with four digits are presented without a comma (e.g., 9960 kilometers). For metric numbers greater than four digits, a space is used instead of a comma (e.g., 12 500 liters).

1) When a number is subtracted from 24 and the difference is divided by that number, the result is 3. What is the value of the number?

    A. 2

    B. 4

    C. 6

    D. 12

2) An angle is equal to one fifth of its supplement. What is the measure of that angle?

    A. 20

    B. 30

    C. 45

    D. 60

3) John traveled 150 km in 6 hours and Alice traveled 180 km in 4 hours. What is the ratio of the average speed of John to average speed of Alice?

    A. $3:2$

    B. $2:3$

    C. $5:9$

    D. $5:6$

4) If 40% of a class are girls, and 35% of girls play tennis, what percent of the class play tennis?

    A. 10%

    B. 14%

    C. 20%

    D. 40%

5) If the interior angles of a quadrilateral are in the ratio $1:2:3:4$, what is the measure of the smallest angle?

    A. $36°$

    B. $72°$

    C. $108°$

    D. $144°$

6) How long does a 420–miles trip take moving at 50 miles per hour (*mph*)?

   A. 4 *hours*

   B. 6 *hours and* 24 *minutes*

   C. 8 *hours and* 24 *minutes*

   D. 8 *hours and* 30 *minutes*

7) Right triangle ABC has two legs of lengths 6 *cm* (AB) and 8 *cm* (AC). What is the length of the third side (BC)?

   A. 4 *cm*

   B. 6 *cm*

   C. 8 *cm*

   D. 10 *cm*

8) The ratio of boys to girls in a school is $2 : 3$. If there are 600 students in a school, how many boys are in the school.

   A. 540

   B. 360

   C. 300

   D. 240

9) 25 is What percent of 20?

   A. 20%

   B. 25%

   C. 125%

   D. 150%

10) The perimeter of the trapezoid below is 54. What is its area?

   A. 252 cm^2

   B. 234 cm^2

   C. 216 cm^2

   D. 130 cm^2

11) Two third of 18 is equal to $\frac{2}{5}$ of what number?

   A. 12

   B. 20

   C. 30

   D. 60

12) The marked price of a computer is D dollar. Its price decreased by 20% in January and later increased by 10% in February. What is the final price of the computer in D dollar?

   A. $0.80\ D$

   B. $0.88\ D$

   C. $0.90\ D$

   D. $1.20\ D$

13) The area of a circle is $25\ \pi$. What is the circumference of the circle?

   A. $5\ \pi$

   B. $10\ \pi$

   C. $32\ \pi$

   D. $64\ \pi$

14) In 1999, the average worker's income increased $3,000 per year starting from $24,000 annual salary. Which equation represents income greater than average? (I = income, x = number of years after 1999)

   A. $I > 3,000\ x + 24,000$

   B. $I > -3,000\ x + 24,000$

   C. $I < -3,000\ x + 24,000$

   D. $I < 3,000\ x - 24,000$

15) From last year, the price of gasoline has increased from $1.25 per gallon to $1.75 per gallon. The new price is what percent of the original price?

   A. 72%

   B. 120%

   C. 140%

   D. 160%

16) A boat sails 40 miles south and then 30 miles east. How far is the boat from its start point?

    A. 45 *miles*

    B. 50 *miles*

    C. 60 *miles*

    D. 70 *miles*

17) Sophia purchased a sofa for $530.40. The sofa is regularly priced at $624. What was the percent discount Sophia received on the sofa?

    A. 12%

    B. 15%

    C. 20%

    D. 25%

18) The score of Emma was half as that of Ava and the score of Mia was twice that of Ava. If the score of Mia was 60, what is the score of Emma?

    A. 12

    B. 15

    C. 20

    D. 30

19) The average of five consecutive numbers is 38. What is the smallest number?

    A. 38

    B. 36

    C. 34

    D. 12

20) How many tiles of $8\ cm^2$ is needed to cover a floor of dimension $6\ cm$ by $24\ cm$?

    A. 6

    B. 12

    C. 18

    D. 24

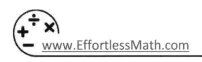

21) A rope weighs 600 grams per meter of length. What is the weight in kilograms of 12.2 meters of this rope? ($1\ kilograms = 1000\ grams$)

   A. 0.0732

   B. 0.732

   C. 7.32

   D. 7,320

22) A chemical solution contains 4% alcohol. If there is $24\ ml$ of alcohol, what is the volume of the solution?

   A. $240\ ml$

   B. $480\ ml$

   C. $600\ ml$

   D. $1,200\ ml$

23) The average weight of 18 girls in a class is $60\ kg$ and the average weight of 32 boys in the same class is $62\ kg$. What is the average weight of all the 50 students in that class?

   A. 60

   B. 61.28

   C. 61.68

   D. 61.90

24) The price of a laptop is decreased by 10% to $360. What is its original price?

   A. $320

   B. $380

   C. $400

   D. $450

25) The radius of a cylinder is 8 inches and its height is 12 inches. What is the surface area of the cylinder?

   A. $64\ \pi\ in^2$

   B. $128\ \pi\ in^2$

   C. $192\ \pi\ in^2$

   D. $320\ \pi\ in^2$

26) The average of $13, 15, 20$ and x is 18. What is the value of x?

    A. 9

    B. 15

    C. 18

    D. 24

27) The price of a sofa is decreased by 25% to $420. What was its original price?

    A. $480

    B. $520

    C. $560

    D. $600

28) A bank is offering 4.5% simple interest on a savings account. If you deposit $8,000, how much interest will you earn in five years?

    A. $360

    B. $720

    C. $1,800

    D. $3,600

29) Multiply and write the product in scientific notation:

$$(4.2 \times 10^6) \times (2.6 \times 10^{-5})$$

    A. 1092×10

    B. 10.92×10^6

    C. 109.2×10^{-5}

    D. 1.092×10^2

30) If the height of a right pyramid is $12\ cm$ and its base is a square with side $6\ cm$. What is its volume?

    A. $32\ cm^3$

    B. $36\ cm^3$

    C. $48\ cm^3$

    D. $144\ cm^3$

31) Solve for x: $4(x + 1) = 6(x - 4) + 20$

   A. 12

   B. 8

   C. 6.2

   D. 4

32) Which of the following expressions is equivalent to $2x(4 + 2y)$?

   A. $2xy + 8x$

   B. $8xy + 8x$

   C. $xy + 8$

   D. $4xy + 8x$

33) If $y = 4ab + 3b^3$, what is y when $a = 2$ and $b = 3$?

   A. 24

   B. 31

   C. 36

   D. 105

34) Which of the following graphs represents the compound inequality $-2 \le 2x - 4 < 8$?

   A.

   B.

   C.

   D.

35) A number is chosen at random from 1 to 25. Find the probability of not selecting a composite number.

   A. $\dfrac{9}{25}$

   B. 25

   C. $\dfrac{2}{5}$

   D. 1

36) Which of the following points lies on the line $2x + 4y = 10$

   A. $(2, 1)$

   B. $(-1, 3)$

   C. $(-2, 2)$

   D. $(2, 2)$

37) The price of a car was $20,000 in 2014, $16,000 in 2015 and $12,800 in 2016. What is the rate of depreciation of the price of car per year?

   A. 15%

   B. 20%

   C. 25%

   D. 30%

38) A ladder leans against a wall forming a $60°$ angle between the ground and the ladder. If the bottom of the ladder is 30 feet away from the wall, how long is the ladder?

   A. $30\ feet$

   B. $40\ feet$

   C. $50\ feet$

   D. $60\ feet$

39) Anita's trick–or–treat bag contains 12 pieces of chocolate, 18 suckers, 18 pieces of gum, 24 pieces of licorice. If she randomly pulls a piece of candy from her bag, what is the probability of her pulling out a piece of sucker?

A. $\dfrac{1}{3}$

B. $\dfrac{1}{4}$

C. $\dfrac{1}{6}$

D. $\dfrac{1}{12}$

40) If $x + y = 0$, $4x - 2y = 24$, which of the following ordered pairs (x, y) satisfies both equations?

A. $(4, 3)$

B. $(5, 4)$

C. $(4, -4)$

D. $(4, -6)$

41) If $f(x) = 3x + 4(x + 1) + 2$ then $f(3x) =$?

A. $21x + 6$

B. $16x - 6$

C. $25x + 4$

D. $12x + 3$

42) A line in the xy-plane passes through origin and has a slope of $\dfrac{2}{3}$. Which of the following points lies on the line?

A. $(2, 1)$

B. $(4, 1)$

C. $(9, 6)$

D. $(9, 3)$

43) Which of the following is equivalent to $(3n^2 + 4n + 6) - (2n^2 - 5)$?

A. $n + 4n^2$

B. $n^2 - 3$

C. $n^2 + 4n + 11$

D. $n + 2$

44) If $(ax + 4)(bx + 3) = 10x^2 + cx + 12$ for all values of x and $a + b = 7$, what are the two

possible values for c?

A. $22, 21$

B. $20, 22$

C. $23, 26$

D. $24, 23$

45) Point A lies on the line with equation $y - 3 = 2(x + 5)$. If the x −coordinate of A is 8, what

is the y −coordinate of A?

A. 14

B. 16

C. 22

D. 29

End of FTCE Mathematics Practice Test 2

FTCE General Knowledge Mathematics Practice Tests
Answer Keys

Now, it's time to review your results to see where you went wrong and what areas you need to improve.

FTCE Math Practice Test 1						FTCE Math Practice Test 2					
1	C	21	D	41	D	1	C	21	C	41	A
2	D	22	D	42	C	2	B	22	C	42	C
3	D	23	B	43	B	3	C	23	B	43	C
4	D	24	A	44	D	4	B	24	C	44	C
5	B	25	D	45	C	5	A	25	D	45	D
6	C	26	A			6	C	26	D		
7	D	27	D			7	D	27	C		
8	C	28	B			8	D	28	C		
9	B	29	C			9	C	29	D		
10	D	30	D			10	D	30	D		
11	B	31	C			11	C	31	D		
12	D	32	C			12	B	32	D		
13	C	33	D			13	B	33	D		
14	D	34	D			14	A	34	D		
15	B	35	D			15	C	35	C		
16	B	36	B			16	B	36	B		
17	D	37	D			17	B	37	B		
18	A	38	D			18	B	38	D		
19	C	39	C			19	B	39	B		
20	D	40	A			20	C	40	C		

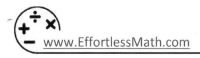

FTCE General Knowledge Math Practice Tests Answers and Explanations

FTCE Math Practice Test 1

1) Choice C is correct

$$average\ (mean) = \frac{sum\ of\ terms}{number\ of\ terms} \Rightarrow 90 = \frac{sum\ of\ terms}{50} \Rightarrow sum = 90 \times 50 = 4,500$$

The difference of 94 and 69 is 25. Therefore, 25 should be subtracted from the sum.

$$4,500 - 25 = 4,475,\ mean = \frac{sum\ of\ terms}{number\ of\ terms} \Rightarrow mean = \frac{4,475}{50} = 89.5$$

2) Choice D is correct

For sum of 5: $(1\ \&\ 4)\ and\ (4\ \&\ 1), (2\ \&\ 3)$ and $(3\ \&\ 2)$, therefore we have 4 options.

For sum of 8: $(5\ \&\ 3)and\ (3\ \&\ 5), (4\ \&\ 4)$ and $(2\ \&\ 6)$, and $(6\ \&\ 2)$,we have 5 options. To get a sum of 5 or 8 for two dice: $4 + 5 = 9$.Since, we have $6 \times 6 = 36$ total number of options, the

probability of getting a sum of 5 and 8 is 9 out of 36 or $\frac{9}{36} = \frac{1}{4}$

3) Choice D is correct

Use FOIL method. $(5x + 2y)(2x - y) = 10x^2 - 5xy + 4xy - 2y^2 = 10x^2 - xy - 2y^2$

4) Choice D is correct

To solve absolute values equations, write two equations. $x - 10$ could be positive 4, or negative 4. Therefore, $x - 10 = 4 \Rightarrow x = 14$, $x - 10 = -4 \Rightarrow x = 6$. Find the product of solutions: $6 \times 14 = 84$

5) Choice B is correct

The equation of a line in slope intercept form is: $y = mx + b$. Solve for y.

$4x - 2y = 6 \Rightarrow -2y = 6 - 4x \Rightarrow y = (6 - 4x) \div (-2) \Rightarrow y = 2x - 3$. The slope is 2.

The slope of the line perpendicular to this line is: $m_1 \times m_2 = -1 \Rightarrow 2 \times m_2 = -1 \Rightarrow m_2 = -\frac{1}{2}$.

6) Choice C is correct

Plug in the value of x and y. $x = 3$ and $y = -2$.

$$6(x - 2y) + (2 - x)^2 = 6(3 - 2(-2)) + (2 - 3)^2 = 6(3 + 4) + (-1)^2 = 42 + 1 = 43$$

7) Choice D is correct

Use formula of rectangle prism volume. $V = (length)(width)(height) \Rightarrow 2,500 = (25)(10)(height) \Rightarrow height = 2,500 \div 250 = 10$

8) Choice C is correct

$$4 \div \frac{1}{3} = 12$$

9) Choice B is correct

The diagonal of the square is 4. Let x be the side. Use Pythagorean Theorem: $a^2 + b^2 = c^2$

$$x^2 + x^2 = 4^2 \Rightarrow 2x^2 = 4^2 \Rightarrow 2x^2 = 16 \Rightarrow x^2 = 8 \Rightarrow x = \sqrt{8}$$

The area of the square is: $\sqrt{8} \times \sqrt{8} = 8$

10) Choice D is correct

Solve for the sum of five numbers.

$$average = \frac{sum\ of\ terms}{number\ of\ terms} \Rightarrow 26 = \frac{sum\ of\ 5\ numbers}{5} \Rightarrow sum\ of\ 5\ numbers = 26 \times 5 = 130$$

The sum of 5 numbers is 130. If a sixth number 42 is added, then the sum of 6 numbers is

$$130 + 42 = 172.\ average = \frac{sum\ of\ terms}{number\ of\ terms} = \frac{172}{6} = 28.66$$

11) Choice B is correct

ratio of A: $\frac{570}{600} = 0.95$ ratio of B: $\frac{291}{300} = 0.97$ ratio of C: $\frac{665}{700} = 0.95$ ratio of D: $\frac{528}{550} = 0.96$

The maximum ratio is 0.97.

12) Choice D is correct

First find percentage of men in city A and percentage of women in city C. Percentage of men in city A $= \frac{600}{1,170}$ and percentage of women in city C $= \frac{665}{1,365}$. Find the ratio and simplify. $\frac{\frac{600}{1,170}}{\frac{665}{1,365}} = \frac{20}{19}$

13) Choice C is correct

$\frac{528 + x}{550} = 1.2 \rightarrow 528 + x = 660 \rightarrow x = 132$

14) Choice D is correct

Jason needs an 70% average to pass for five exams. Therefore, the sum of 5 exams must be at lease $5 \times 70 = 350$. The sum of 4 exams is: $68 + 72 + 85 + 90 = 315$.

The minimum score Jason can earn on his fifth and final test to pass is: $350 - 315 = 35$

15) Choice B is correct

Isolate and solve for x. $\frac{2}{3}x + \frac{1}{6} = \frac{1}{2} \Rightarrow \frac{2}{3}x = \frac{1}{2} - \frac{1}{6} = \frac{1}{3} \Rightarrow \frac{2}{3}x = \frac{1}{3}$. Multiply both sides by the reciprocal of the coefficient of x. $(\frac{3}{2})\frac{1}{3}x = \frac{1}{3}(\frac{3}{2}) \Rightarrow x = \frac{3}{6} = \frac{1}{2}$

16) Choice B is correct

Use simple interest formula: $I = prt$ ($I =$ interest, $p =$ principal, $r =$ rate, $t =$ time).

$$I = (12,000)(0.045)(2) = 1,080$$

17) Choice D is correct

Simplify. $7x^2 y^3 (2x^2 y)^3 = 7x^2 y^3 (8x^6 y^3) = 56x^8 y^6$

18) Choice A is correct

Surface Area of a cylinder $= 2\pi r (r + h)$, The radius of the cylinder is 2 ($4 \div 2$) inches and its height is 8 inches. Therefore, Surface Area of a cylinder $= 2\pi (2)(2 + 8) = 40\pi$

19) Choice C is correct

Three times of 25,000 is 75,000. One sixth of them cancelled their tickets. One sixth of 75,000 equals 12,500 ($\frac{1}{6} \times 75{,}000 = 12{,}500$). 62,500 ($75{,}000 - 12{,}000 = 62{,}500$) fans are attending this week.

20) Choice D is correct

The area of the square is 49 inches. Therefore, the side of the square is square root of the area.

$\sqrt{49} = 7$ inches. Four times the side of the square is the perimeter: $4 \times 7 = 28 \; inches$

21) Choice D is correct

$g(x) = -4$, then $f\big(g(x)\big) = f(-4) = 2\,(-4)^3 + 5(-4)^2 + 2(-4) = -128 + 80 - 8 = -56$

22) Choice D is correct

Use the information provided in the question to draw the shape.

Use Pythagorean Theorem: $a^2 + b^2 = c^2$

$50^2 + 120^2 = c^2 \Rightarrow 2{,}500 + 14{,}400 = c^2 \Rightarrow 16{,}900 = c^2 \Rightarrow c = 130$

120 miles

Port A

50 miles

23) Choice B is correct

Plug in 104 for F and then solve for C.

$C = \dfrac{5}{9}\,(F - 32) \Rightarrow C = \dfrac{5}{9}\,(104 - 32) \Rightarrow C = \dfrac{5}{9}\,(72) = 40$

24) Choice A is correct

The width of the rectangle is twice its length. Let x be the length. Then, $width = 2x$

Perimeter of the rectangle is $2\,(width + length) = 2(2x + x) = 72 \Rightarrow 6x = 72 \Rightarrow x = 12$. Length of the rectangle is 12 meters.

25) Choice D is correct

$average = \dfrac{sum\ of\ terms}{number\ of\ terms} \Rightarrow$ (average of 6 numbers) $14 = \dfrac{sum\ of\ numbers}{6} \Rightarrow$ sum of

6 numbers

is $14 \times 6 = 84$, (average of 4 numbers) $10 = \frac{\text{sum of numbers}}{4}$ ⇒sum of 4 numbers is $10 \times 4 = 40$. *sum of 6 numbers − sum of 4 numbers = sum of 2 numbers,*

$84 - 40 = 44$ average of 2 numbers $= \frac{44}{2} = 22$

26) Choice A is correct

First, find the number. Let x be the number. Write the equation and solve for x. 150% of a number is 75, then:$1.5 \times x = 75 \Rightarrow x = 75 \div 1.5 = 50$, 80% of 50 is: $0.8 \times 50 = 40$

27) Choice D is correct

Solve for y. $4x - 2y = 12 \Rightarrow -2y = 12 - 4x \Rightarrow y = 2x - 6$. The slope of the line is 2.

28) Choice B is correct

the population is increased by 10% and 20%. 10% increase changes the population to 110% of original population. For the second increase, multiply the result by 120%.

$(1.10) \times (1.20) = 1.32 = 132\%$. 32 percent of the population is increased after two years.

29) Choice C is correct

The formula for the area of the circle is: $A = \pi r^2$,The area is 36π. Therefore:$A = \pi r^2 \Rightarrow 6\pi = \pi r^2$, Divide both sides by π: $36 = r^2 \Rightarrow r = 6$. Diameter of a circle is $2 \times$ radius. Then:

Diameter $= 2 \times 6 = 12$

30) Choice D is correct

If 20% of a number is 4, what is the number: 20% *of* $x = 4 \Rightarrow 0.20\, x = 4 \Rightarrow x = 4 \div 0.20 = 20$

31) Choice C is correct

Write a proportion and solve for x.$\frac{3}{2} = \frac{x}{26} \Rightarrow 2x = 3 \times 26 \Rightarrow x = 39\ ft$

32) Choice C is correct

The distance between Jason and Joe is 9 *miles*. Jason running at 6.5 *miles per hour* and Joe is running at the speed of 8 *miles per hour*. Therefore, every hour the distance is 1.5 *miles* less.

$9 \div 1.5 = 6$

33) Choice D is correct

The failing rate is 11 out of $44 = \frac{11}{44}$, Change the fraction to percent: $\frac{11}{44} \times 100\% = 25\%$. 25 percent of students failed. Therefore, 75 percent of students passed the exam.

34) Choice D is correct

$g(x) = -3$, then $f\big(g(x)\big) = $ f$(-3) = 2\,(-3)^3 + 5(-3)^2 + 2(-3) = -54 + 45 - 6 = -15$

35) Choice D is correct

Let x be the width of the rectangle. Use Pythagorean Theorem:

$a^2 + b^2 = c^2$

$x^{\,2} + 6^{\,2} = 10^{\,2} \Rightarrow x^2 + 36 = 100 \Rightarrow x^2 = 100 - 36 = 64 \Rightarrow x = 8$

Perimeter of the rectangle $= 2\,(length \ + \ width) = 2\,(8 \ + \ 6) \ = \ 2\,(14) \ = \ 28$

36) Choice B is correct

The perimeter of the trapezoid is 40.herefore, the missing side (height) is

$= 40 - 8 - 12 - 6 = 14$. Area of a trapezoid: $A \ = \ \frac{1}{2}\,h\,(b_1 \ + \ b_2) \ = \ \frac{1}{2}\,(14)\,(6 + 8) \ = 98$

37) Choice D is correct

$$f\big(g(x)\big) = 2 \times (\frac{1}{x})^3 + 2 = \frac{2}{x^3} + 2$$

38) Choice D is correct

Use the information provided in the question to draw the shape.

Use Pythagorean Theorem: $a^2 + b^2 = c^2$

$80^2 + 150^2 = c^2 \Rightarrow 6{,}400 + 22{,}500 = c^2 \Rightarrow 28{,}900 = c^2 \Rightarrow$ c $= 170$

39) Choice C is correct

Write the ratio of $5a$ to $2b$. $\frac{5a}{2b} = \frac{1}{10}$. Use cross multiplication and then simplify.

$$5a \times 10 = 2b \times 1 \rightarrow 50a = 2b \rightarrow a = \frac{2b}{50} = \frac{b}{25}$$

Now, find the ratio of a to b. $\dfrac{a}{b} = \dfrac{\frac{b}{25}}{b} \rightarrow \dfrac{b}{25} \div b = \dfrac{b}{25} \times \dfrac{1}{b} = \dfrac{b}{25b} = \dfrac{1}{25}$

40) Choice A is correct

Plug in the value of x in the equation and solve for y. $2y = \dfrac{2x^2}{3} + 6 \rightarrow 2y = \dfrac{2(9)^2}{3} + 6 \rightarrow$

$$2y = \dfrac{2(81)}{3} + 6 \rightarrow 2y = 54 + 6 = 60 \rightarrow 2y = 60 \rightarrow y = 30$$

41) Choice D is correct

Since $N = 6$, substitute 6 for N in the equation $\dfrac{x-3}{5} = N$, which gives $\dfrac{x-3}{5} = 6$. Multiplying both

sides of $\dfrac{x-3}{5} = 6$ by 5 gives $x - 3 = 30$ and then adding 3 to both sides of $x - 3 = 30$ then,

$x = 33$.

42) Choice C is correct

$b^{\frac{m}{n}} = \sqrt[n]{b^m}$ For any positive integers m and n. Thus, $b^{\frac{3}{5}} = \sqrt[5]{b^3}$

43) Choice B is correct

The total number of pages read by Sara is 3 (hours she spent reading) multiplied by her rate of

reading: $\dfrac{N pages}{hour} \times 3 hours = 3N$

Similarly, the total number of pages read by Mary is 4 (hours she spent reading) multiplied by her

rate of reading: $\dfrac{M pages}{hour} \times 4 hours = 4M$ the total number of pages read by Sara and Mary is the

sum of the total number of pages read by Sara and the total number of pages read by Mary: $3N +$

$4M$.

44) Choice D is correct

The initial deposit earns 2 percent interest compounded annually. Thus, at the end of year 1, the

new value of the account is the initial deposit of $150 plus 2 percent of the initial deposit:

$\$150 + \dfrac{2}{100}(\$150) = \$150(1.02)$.

Since the interest is compounded annually, the value at the end of each succeeding year is the

sum of the previous year's value plus 2 percent of the previous year's value. This is equivalent to multiplying the previous year's value by 1.02. Thus, after 2 years, the value will be $150(1.02)(1.02) = \$(150)(1.02)^2$; and after 3 years, the value will be $(150)(1.02)^3$; and after n years, the value will be $(150)(1.02)^n$. Therefore, in the formula for the value for Sara's account after n years $(100)(x)^n$, the value of x is 1.02.

45) Choice C is correct

First find the value of b, and then find $f(5)$. Since $f(2) = 35$, substuting 2 for x and 35 for $f(x)$ gives $35 = b(2)^2 + 15 = 4b + 15$. Solving this equation gives $b = 5$. Thus

$$f(x) = 5x^2 + 15, \quad f(5) = 5(5)^2 + 15 \rightarrow f(5) = 125 + 15, \quad f(5) = 140$$

FTCE Math Practice Test 2

1) Choice C is correct

Let x be the number. Write the equation and solve for x. $(24 - x) \div x = 3$. Multiply both sides by x. $(24 - x) = 3x$, then add x both sides. $24 = 4x$, now divide both sides by 4.

$x = 6$

2) Choice B is correct

The sum of supplement angles is 180. Let x be that angle. Therefore, $x + 5x = 180$

$6x = 180$, divide both sides by 6: $x = 30$

3) Choice C is correct

The average speed of john is: $150 \div 6 = 25$, The average speed of Alice is: $180 \div 4 = 45$

Write the ratio and simplify. $25 : 45 \Rightarrow 5 : 9$

4) Choice B is correct

The percent of girls playing tennis is: $40\% \times 35\% = 0.40 \times 0.35 = 0.14 = 14\%$

5) Choice A is correct

The sum of all angles in a quadrilateral is 360 degrees. Let x be the smallest angle in the quadrilateral. Then the angles are: $x, 2x, 3x, 4x$,

$x + 2x + 3x + 4x = 360 \rightarrow 10x = 360 \rightarrow x = 36$, The angles in the quadrilateral are: $36°, 72°, 108°$, and $144°$, The smallest angle is 36 degrees.

6) Choice C is correct

Use distance formula: $Distance = Rate \times time \Rightarrow 420 = 50 \times T$, divide both sides by 50. $420 \div 50 = T \Rightarrow T = 8.4\ hours$.Change hours to minutes for the decimal part. $0.4\ hours = 0.4 \times 60 = 24\ minutes$.

7) Choice D is correct

Use Pythagorean Theorem: $a^2 + b^2 = c^2$, $6^2 + 8^2 = c^2 \Rightarrow 100 = c^2 \Rightarrow c = 10$

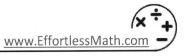

8) Choice D is correct

Th ratio of boy to girls is $2:3$. Therefore, there are 2 boys out of 5 students. To find the answer, first divide the total number of students by 5, then multiply the result by 2.

$$600 \div 5 = 120 \Rightarrow 120 \times 2 = 240$$

9) Choice C is correct

Use percent formula: $part = \frac{percent}{100} \times whole$

$$25 = \frac{percent}{100} \times 20 \Rightarrow 25 = \frac{percent \times 20}{100} \Rightarrow 25$$

$$= \frac{percent \times 2}{10}, multiply\ both\ sides\ by\ 10.$$

$250 = percent \times 2$, divide both sides by 2. $\qquad 125 = percent$

10) Choice D is correct

The perimeter of the trapezoid is 54.

Therefore, the missing side (height) is $= 54 - 18 - 12 - 14 = 10$

Area of the trapezoid: $A = \frac{1}{2} h (b_1 + b_2) = \frac{1}{2} (10) (12 + 14) = 130$

11) Choice C is correct

Let x be the number. Write the equation and solve for x. $\frac{2}{3} \times 18 = \frac{2}{5} . x \Rightarrow \frac{2 \times 18}{3} = \frac{2x}{5}$, use

cross multiplication to solve for x. $5 \times 36 = 2x \times 3 \Rightarrow 180 - 6x \Rightarrow x = 30$

12) Choice B is correct

To find the discount, multiply the number by $(100\% - rate\ of\ discount)$.

Therefore, for the first discount we get: $(D) (100\% - 20\%) = (D) (0.80) = 0.80\ D$

For increase of 10%: $(0.80\ D)(100\% + 10\%) = (0.80\ D)(1.10) = 0.88\ D = 88\%\ of\ D$

13) Choice B is correct

Use the formula of areas of circles. $Area = \pi r^2 \Rightarrow 25 \pi = \pi r^2 \Rightarrow 25 = r^2 \Rightarrow r = 5$

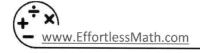

Radius of the circle is 5. Now, use the circumference formula: Circumference $= 2\pi r = 2\pi(5) = 10\pi$

14) Choice A is correct

Let x be the number of years. Therefore, $3,000 per year equals $2,000x$. starting from $24,000 annual salary means you should add that amount to $3,000x$. Income more than that is:

$I > 3,000\,x + 24,000$

15) Choice C is correct

The question is this: 1.75 is what percent of 1.25? Use percent formula: $part = \frac{percent}{100} \times whole$

$$1.75 = \frac{percent}{100} \times 1.25 \Rightarrow 1.75 = \frac{percent \times 1.25}{100} \Rightarrow 175 = percent \times 1.25$$

$$\Rightarrow percent = \frac{175}{1.25} = 140$$

16) Choice B is correct

Use the information provided in the question to draw the shape.

Use Pythagorean Theorem: $a^2 + b^2 = c^2$

$40^2 + 30^2 = c^2 \Rightarrow 1600 + 900 = c^2 \Rightarrow 2500 = c^2 \Rightarrow c = 50$

40 miles

30 miles

17) Choice B is correct

The question is this: 530.40 is what percent of 624?

Use percent formula: $part = \frac{percent}{100} \times whole$. $530.40 = \frac{percent}{100} \times 624 \Rightarrow$

$$530.40 = \frac{percent \times 624}{100} \Rightarrow 53040 = percent \times 624 \Rightarrow percent = \frac{530.40}{624} = 85$$

530.40 is 85% of 624. Therefore, the discount is: $100\% - 85\% = 15\%$

18) Choice B is correct

If the score of Mia was 60, therefore the score of Ava is 30. Since, the score of Emma was half as that of Ava, therefore, the score of Emma is 15.

19) Choice B is correct

Let x be the smallest number. Then, these are the numbers: $x, x + 1, x + 2, x + 3, x + 4$

$$average = \frac{sum\ of\ terms}{number\ of\ terms} \Rightarrow 38 = \frac{x + (x + 1) + (x + 2) + (x + 3) + (x + 4)}{5} \Rightarrow 38$$

$$= \frac{5x + 10}{5} \Rightarrow 190 = 5x + 10 \Rightarrow 180 = 5x \Rightarrow x = 36$$

20) Choice C is correct

The area of the floor is: $6\ cm \times 24\ cm = 144\ cm^2$, The number is tiles needed =

$$144 \div 8 = 18$$

21) Choice C is correct

The weight of 12.2 meters of this rope is: $12.2 \times 600\ g = 7,320\ g$,

$1\ kg = 1,000\ g$, therefore, $7,320\ g \div 1,000 = 7.32\ kg$

22) Choice C is correct

4% of the volume of the solution is alcohol. Let x be the volume of the solution.

Then: $4\%\ of\ x = 24\ ml \Rightarrow 0.04\ x = 24 \Rightarrow x = 24 \div 0.04 = 600$

23) Choice B is correct

$average = \frac{sum\ of\ terms}{number\ of\ terms}$, The sum of the weight of all girls is: $18 \times 60 = 1,080\ kg$, The sum of the weight of all boys is: $32 \times 62 = 1,984\ kg$, The sum of the weight of all students is: $1,080 + 1,984 = 3,064\ kg$, average $= \frac{3,064}{50} = 61.28$

24) Choice C is correct

Let x be the original price. If the price of a laptop is decreased by 10% to $360, then: $90\%\ of\ x = 360 \Rightarrow 0.90x = 360 \Rightarrow x = 360 \div 0.90 = 400$

25) Choice D is correct

Surface Area of a cylinder $= 2\pi r\ (r + h)$, The radius of the cylinder is 8 inches and its height is 12 inches. Surface Area of a cylinder $= 2\ (\pi)\ (8)\ (8 + 12) = 320\ \pi$

26) Choice D is correct

$$average = \frac{sum\ of\ terms}{number\ of\ terms} \Rightarrow 18 = \frac{13 + 15 + 20 + x}{4} \Rightarrow 72 = 48 + x \Rightarrow x = 24$$

27) Choice C is correct

Let x be the original price. If the price of the sofa is decreased by 25% to $420, then: 75% $of\ x = 420 \Rightarrow 0.75x = 420 \Rightarrow x = 420 \div 0.75 = 560$

28) Choice C is correct

Use simple interest formula: $I = prt$, (I = interest, p = principal, r = rate, t = time)

$$I = (8,000)(0.045)(5) = 1,800$$

29) Choice D is correct

$$(4.2 \times 10^6) \times (2.6 \times 10^{-5}) = (4.2 \times 2.6) \times (10^6 \times 10^{-5}) = 10.92 \times (10^{6 + (-5)})$$
$$= 1.092 \times 10^2$$

30) Choice D is correct

The formula of the volume of pyramid is: $V = \frac{l \times w \times h}{3}$. The length and width of the pyramid is $6\ cm$ and its height is $12\ cm$. Therefore: $V = \frac{6 \times 6 \times 12}{3} = 144\ cm^3$

31) Choice D is correct

Simplify: $4(x + 1) = 6(x - 4) + 20, 4x + 4 = 6x - 24 + 20, 4x + 4 = 6x - 4$

Subtract $4x$ from both sides: $4 = 2x - 4$, Add 4 to both sides: $8 = 2x, 4 = x$

32) Choice D is correct

Use distributive property: $2x(4 + 2y) = 8x + 4xy = 4xy + 8x$

33) Choice D is correct

$y = 4ab + 3b^3$, plug in the values of a and b in the equation: $a = 2$ and $b = 3$,

$$y = 4ab + 3b^3 \rightarrow y = 4(2)(3) + 3(3^3) = 24 + 81 = 105$$

34) Choice D is correct

Solve for x. $-2 \leq 2x - 4 < 8 \Rightarrow$ (add 4 all sides) $-2 + 4 \leq 2x - 4 + 4 < 8 + 4 \Rightarrow$

$2 \leq 2x < 12 \Rightarrow$ (divide all sides by 2) $1 \leq x < 6$

x is between 1 and 6. Choice D represent this inequality.

35) Choice C is correct

Set of number that are not composite between 1 and 25: A= {1, 2, 3, 5, 7, 11, 13, 17, 19, 23}

$$Probability = \frac{number\ of\ desired\ outcomes}{number\ of\ total\ outcomes} = \frac{10}{25} = \frac{2}{5}$$

36) Choice B is correct

Plug in each pair of number in the equation:

A. $(2, 1)$: $2\,(2) + 4\,(1) = 8$

B. $(-1, 3)$: $2\,(-1) + 4\,(3) = 10$

C. $(-2, 2)$: $2\,(-2) + 4\,(2) = 4$

D. $(2, 2)$: $2\,(2) + 4\,(2) = 12$

Only Choice B is correct.

37) Choice B is correct

Use this formula: Percent of Change: $\dfrac{New\ Value - Old\ Value}{Old\ Value} \times 100\%$

$\dfrac{16,000 - 20,000}{20,000} \times 100\% = -20\%$ and $\dfrac{12,800 - 16,000}{16,000} \times 100\ \% = -20\%$

38) Choice D is correct

The relationship among all sides of special right triangle

$30° - 60° - 90°$ is provided in this triangle:

In this triangle, the opposite side of $30°$ angle is half of the hypotenuse.

Draw the shape of this question:

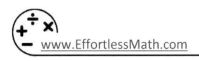

The ladder is the hypotenuse. Therefore, the ladder is $60 \ ft$

39) Choice B is correct

$$Probability = \frac{number \ of \ desired \ outcomes}{number \ of \ total \ outcomes} = \frac{18}{12 + 18 + 18 + 24} = \frac{18}{72} = \frac{1}{4}$$

40) Choice C is correct

Method 1: Plugin the values of x and y provided in the options into both equations.

A. $(4, 3)$ $x + y = 0 \rightarrow 4 + 3 \neq 0$

B. $(5, 4)$ $x + y = 0 \rightarrow 5 + 4 \neq 0$

C. $(4, -4)$ $x + y = 0 \rightarrow 4 + (-4) = 0$

D. $(4, -6)$ $x + y = 0 \rightarrow 4 + (-6) \neq 0$

Only option C is correct.

Method 2: Multiplying each side of $x + y = 0$ by 2 gives $2x + 2y = 0$. Then, adding the corresponding side of $2x + 2y = 0$ and $4x - 2y = 24$ gives $6x = 24$. Dividing each side of $6x = 24$ by 6 gives $x = 4$. Finally, substituting 4 for x in $x + y = 0$, or $y = -4$. Therefore, the solution to the given system of equations is $(4, -4)$.

41) Choice A is correct

If $f(x) = 3x + 4(x + 1) + 2$, then find $f(3x)$ by substituting $3x$ for every x in the function. This gives: $f(3x) = 3 (3x) + 4(3x + 1) + 2$

It simplifies to: $f(3x) = 3 (3x) + 4(3x + 1) + 2 = 9x + 12x + 4 + 2 = 21x + 6$

42) Choice C is correct

First, find the equation of the line. All lines through the origin are of the form $y = mx$, so the equation is $y = \frac{2}{3}x$. Of the given choices, only choice C $(9,6)$, satisfies this equation:

$$y = \frac{2}{3}x \rightarrow 6 = \frac{2}{3}(9) = 6$$

43) Choice C is correct

$(3n^2 + 4n + 6) - (2n^2 - 5)$.   Add like terms together: $3n^2 - 2n^2 = n^2$

$4n$ doesn't have like terms. $6 - (-5) = 11$

Combine these terms into one expression to find the answer: $n^2 + 4n + 11$

44) Choice C is correct

You can find the possible values of a and b in $(ax + 4)(bx + 3)$ by using the given equation $a + b = 7$ and finding another equation that relates the variables a and b. Since $(ax + 4)(bx + 3) = 10x^2 + cx + 12$, expand the left side of the equation to obtain

$$abx^2 + 4bx + 3ax + 12 = 10x^2 + cx + 12$$

Since ab is the coefficient of x^2 on the left side of the equation and 10 is the coefficient of x^2 on the right side of the equation, it must be true that $ab = 10$

The coefficient of x on the left side is $4b + 3a$ and the coefficient of x in the right side is c. Then: $4b + 3a = c, \quad a + b = 7$, then: $a = 7 - b$

Now, plug in the value of a in the equation $ab = 10$. Then:

$$ab = 10 \rightarrow (7 - b)b = 10 \rightarrow 7b - b^2 = 10$$

Add $-7b + b^2$ both sides. Then: $b^2 - 7b + 10 = 0$

Solve for b using the factoring method. $b^2 - 7b + 10 = 0 \rightarrow (b - 5)(b - 2) = 0$

Thus, either $b = 2$ and $a = 5$, or $b = 5$ and $a = 2$. If $b = 2$ and $a = 5$, then

$4b + 3a = c \rightarrow 4(2) + 3(5) = c \rightarrow c = 23$. If $5 = 2$ and $a = 2$, then, $4b + 3a = c \rightarrow 4(5) + 3(2) = c \rightarrow c = 26$.   Therefore, the two possible values for c are 23 and 26.

45) Choice D is correct

Here we can substitute 8 for x in the equation. Thus, $y - 3 = 2(8 + 5), \quad y - 3 = 26$

Adding 3 to both side of the equation: $y = 26 + 3, \quad y = 29$

... So Much More Online!

Effortless Math Online FTCE General Knowledge Math Center offers a complete study program, including the following:

✓ Step-by-step instructions on how to prepare for the FTCE General Knowledge Math test

✓ Numerous FTCE General Knowledge Math worksheets to help you measure your math skills

✓ Complete list of FTCE General Knowledge Math formulas

✓ Video lessons for FTCE General Knowledge Math topics

✓ Full-length FTCE General Knowledge Math practice tests

✓ And much more...

No Registration Required.

Visit **EffortlessMath.com/FTCE** to find your online FTCE Math resources.

Receive the PDF version of this book or get another FREE book!

Thank you for using our Book!

Do you LOVE this book?

Then, you can get the PDF version of this book or another book absolutely FREE!

Please email us at:

info@EffortlessMath.com

for details.

Author's Final Note

I hope you enjoyed reading this book. You've made it through the book! Great job!

First of all, thank you for purchasing this study guide. I know you could have picked any number of books to help you prepare for your FTCE General Knowledge Math test, but you picked this book and for that I am extremely grateful.

It took me years to write this study guide for the FTCE General Knowledge Math because I wanted to prepare a comprehensive FTCE General Knowledge Math study guide to help test takers make the most effective use of their valuable time while preparing for the test.

After teaching and tutoring math courses for over a decade, I've gathered my personal notes and lessons to develop this study guide. It is my greatest hope that the lessons in this book could help you prepare for your test successfully.

If you have any questions, please contact me at reza@effortlessmath.com and I will be glad to assist. Your feedback will help me to greatly improve the quality of my books in the future and make this book even better. Furthermore, I expect that I have made a few minor errors somewhere in this study guide. If you think this to be the case, please let me know so I can fix the issue as soon as possible.

If you enjoyed this book and found some benefit in reading this, I'd like to hear from you and hope that you could take a quick minute to post a review on the book's Amazon page. To leave your valuable feedback, please visit: amzn.to/3cws3T5

Or scan this QR code.

I personally go over every single review, to make sure my books really are reaching out and helping students and test takers. Please help me help FTCE General Knowledge Math test takers, by leaving a review!

I wish you all the best in your future success!

Reza Nazari

Math teacher and author

Made in the USA
Columbia, SC
05 May 2022